quick & easy
asian vegetarian
recipes

nutritious and delicious alternatives

Your guide to the exciting world of Asian vegetarian cooking.
Contains over 75 flavorful recipes that can be prepared at home
in minutes, thanks to the simple step-by-step instructions.
A quick trip to your local supermarket is all you need to get started.

PERIPLUS

Contents

MAIL ORDER SOURCES

Finding the ingredients for Asian home cooking has become very simple. Most super-markets carry staples such as soy sauce, fresh ginger, and fresh lemongrass. Almost every large metropolitan area has Asian markets serving the local population—just check your local business directory. With the Internet, exotic Asian ingredients and cooking utensils can be easily found online. The following list is a good starting point of online merchants offering a wide variety of goods and services.

http://www.asiafoods.com

http://www.geocities.com/MadisonAvenue/8074/VarorE.html

http://dmoz.org/Shopping/Food/Ethnic_and_Regional/Asian/

http://templeofthai.com/

http://www.orientalpantry.com/

http://www.zestyfoods.com/

http://www.thaigrocer.com/Merchant/index.htm

http://asianwok.com/

http://pilipinomart.com/

http://www.indiangrocerynet.com/

http://www.orientalfoodexpress.com/

V egetarian cooking has long been an integral part of Asia's culinary land-scape, with many groups of peoples in India, China, Thailand, Vietnam, Korea and other parts of Asia foregoing meat primarily due to religious reasons. This book presents a mouthwatering selection of vegetarian recipes drawn from many different regions of Asia—which are not only extremely nutritious but also simple to prepare and fabulously tasty!

Asian vegetarian cooking differs greatly from the vegetarian fare normally found in Western countries. Extensive use is made of fresh tropical spices, fragrant herbs, exotic vegetables and fruits. Foremost among these are the spicy chili pepper used to impart a pungent bite to many Asian dishes. Sesame oil, toasted sesame seeds or sesame paste, garlic, ginger, galangal, black pepper, fermented black beans and soy sauce are essential ingredients in any Asian larder. And herbs like Asian basil, curry leaves, coriander leaves (cilantro) and mint add zest to sauces and stir-fries, or a bright splash of color when used as a garnish.

Two mainstays of the vegetarian diet in Asia are protein-rich tofu (bean curd) and dried or fresh black Chinese mushrooms. Tofu comes in a wide variety of forms and flavors, and is prepared in an incredible number of different ways—eaten plain with soy sauce and pickled daikon radish, deep-fried with garlic and a bit of salt, "crinkle-fried" with vegetables, stir-fried with seasonings—the list goes on and on. Black Chinese mushrooms have a similar versatility, as well as an exceptionally high nutritional content, and Chinese or Japanese vegetarian meals would be unthinkable without them.

The sheer variety of vegetables found in Asia is incredible, and over many centuries, Asians have developed endless ways of preparing them—each more delicious than the last! All the usual Western vegetables such as cabbage, spinach, potatoes, tomatoes, carrots, etc., are widely eaten, but so are many less common ones like lotus root, mung bean sprouts, bok choy, *choy sum*, water spinach (*kangkong*), and so forth. One of the most exciting things about Asian cooking is exploring the new tastes and textures these unusual vegetables provide. And so many of them are now available in health food stores or Asian food shops!

The staples of an Asian vegetarian meal are rice or noodles combined with some sort of sauce. Indian vegetable curries generally feature a range of protein-rich beans and peas, cooked in half a dozen or more flavorful spices—often with coconut milk or tamarind added. Rice is of course eaten plain with other side dishes and condiments, or prepared in various ways with spices and herbs.

While millions of Asians are vegetarians for religious reasons, there are a growing number who practise it due to health concerns or as a lifestyle choice. As a result, nowhere else in the world is vegetarianism so widespread, and nowhere else can you find such a variety of delicious vegetarian recipes!

Ingredients Glossary

Asian eggplants are long and slender, smaller and milder than Mediterranean globe eggplants. They can be either purple or green.

Asafoetida is a pungent gum which is usually sold in powdered form. Use very small amounts—a pinch is enough. Keep well sealed when not in use.

Bamboo shoots are the fresh shoots of the bamboo plant. Pre-cooked bamboo shoots, packed in water, can be found in the refrigerated section of supermarkets. Canned bamboo shoots are also pre-cooked but should be boiled for 5 minutes to refresh before using.

Black Chinese mushrooms, also known as shiitake mushrooms, are used widely in Asian cooking. The dried ones must be soaked in hot water to soften before use, from 15 minutes to an hour, depending on the thickness.

The stems are removed and discarded; only the caps are used. Fresh shiitake mushroom stems can be eaten if the bottoms are trimmed. Substitute with porcini mushrooms. Fresh shiitake are increasingly available in supermarkets.

Bok choy is a highly nutritious variety of cabbage with long, crisp stalks and spinach-like leaves. It has a clean, slightly peppery flavor and is a wonderful addition to soups and stir-fries. It is available in most well-stocked supermarkets.

Cardamom pods are highly aromatic and contain tiny black seeds. If whole pods are used, they should be removed from the food before serving. If only the seeds are called for, lightly smash the pods and remove the seeds, discarding the pods. **Ground cardamon** is sold in packets or tins.

Fresh finger-length chilies

Dried finger-length chilies

Chili peppers come in many shapes, sizes and colors. Fresh green and red Asian **finger-length chilies** are moderately hot. **Dried chilies** are usually deseeded, cut into lengths and soaked in warm water to soften before use. **Ground red pepper**, also known as cayenne pepper, is a pungent red powder made from ground dried chilies. Substitute dried red chili flakes or chili paste. **Chili oil** is made from dried chilies or chili powder infused in oil, which is used to enliven some Sichuan dishes. **Chili paste** consists of pounded fresh or dried chilies, sometimes mixed with vinegar and garlic and sold in jars.

Chinese celery is much smaller with thinner stems than normal Western celery, and has a very intense, parsley-like flavor. The leaves and sometimes the stems are added to soups, rice dishes and stir-fried vegetables. This type of celery is obtainable in Asian specialty stores. Use celery leaves or Italian parsley as a substitute.

Coconut milk is available canned or in packets in most well-stocked supermarkets. It comes in varying consistencies and you will need to adjust the thickness by adding water as needed. In general, you should add 1 cup of water to 1 cup of coconut cream to obtain thick coconut milk, and 2 cups of water to 1 cup of coconut cream to obtain thin coconut milk.

Coriander is an indispensable herb and spice in Asian cooking. **Coriander seeds** are roasted and then ground in spice pastes. **Coriander roots** are used in the same way, while

coriander leaves (also known as cilantro or Chinese parsley) are used as a herb and a garnish.

Curry leaves are sold in sprigs containing 8–15 small, green leaves and are used to flavor Indian curries. There is no good substitute.

Daikon radish is a large, crisp, white-fleshed root with a sweet and clean flavor. It is widely used in Chinese and Japanese cooking and can be eaten raw or cooked. The skin needs to be peeled and scrubbed before using. Used mainly in soups and stir-fries, it is available in Asian markets and any well-stocked supermarket.

Enokitaki (golden mushrooms) are clusters of slender, cream-colored stalks

with tiny caps, and are available fresh and tinned. The tough ends of the enokitaki should be discarded before use.

Galangal is similar in appearance to ginger and a member of the same family. This aromatic root has a distinctive flavor that is used in dishes throughout Asia. Dried galangal lacks the fragrance of fresh galangal, so try to buy it fresh. It can be sliced and kept sealed in the freezer for several months.

Garam masala is an Indian blend of powdered spices, usually including cinnamon, cardamon, cloves, fennel, black pepper and salt. Pre-blended garam masala can be bought from any store specializing in spices. Store in an airtight jar away from heat or sunlight.

Ghee is a rich clarified butter oil with the milk solids removed and is the main oil used in Indian cooking.

Channa dal

Tur dal

Mung dal

Urad dal or
blackgram dal

Masoor dal

Dal refers to a wide variety of split peas and pulses. **Channa dal** or Bengal gram resembles a yellow split pea but is smaller. Channa dal is also ground to make **Channa flour**. **Masoor dal** are skinned and split lentils. They're salmon-colored, cook quickly, and turn golden and mushy when cooked. **Mung dal** are pale yellow and slightly elongated. **Tur dal** are pale yellow lentil which is smaller than channa dal. **Urad dal** or blackgram dal are sold either with their black skins on or husked, when they are creamy white in color.

Substitute with vegetable oil or butter.

Hoisin sauce or Peking duck sauce is a sweet and spicy reddish-brown sauce made from soybeans, garlic, pepper and various spices. It is commonly used as a dipping sauce for pork and duck dishes, and as a flavoring in stews.

Kaffir lime leaves are used in soups and curries of Thai, Malay or Indonesian origin. They are also thinly sliced and used as a garnish. Buy them fresh, frozen or dried—fresh or frozen leaves are much more fragrant.

Lotus root has a crunchy texture and a beautiful lacy pattern when sliced cross-wise. The long roots are sold fresh in Asian grocery stores, often wrapped in dried mud to keep them moist. They are also available frozen and pre-sliced in plastic packets, or canned. Fresh lotus root must be peeled before using. Substitute jicama.

Palm sugar is made from the distilled juice of various palm fruits and varies in color from golden to dark brown. It has a rich flavor similar to dark brown sugar or maple syrup, which make good substitutes.

Rice wine or **sake** adds a sweet, subtle flavor to dishes. It is widely available in Asian grocery stores and the specialty food sections of supermarkets. Dry sherry is a good substitute.

Sesame paste is made from ground, roasted sesame

Soft tofu

Tofu skin

Dried sweet tofu strips (*tau kee*)

Firm tofu

Pressed tofu
(*tau kwa*)

Tofu or bean curd comes in various forms. **Soft tofu** is silky and smooth but difficult to cook because it falls apart. **Firm tofu** holds its shape well when cut or cooked and has a stronger, slightly sour taste. **Pressed tofu** (often confusingly labeled as firm tofu) is a type of firm tofu that has had much of the moisture extracted and is therefore much firmer in texture and excellent for stir-fries. Refrigerate fresh tofu in a plastic container submerged in water. **Tofu skin** is the dried skin that forms on top of boiling soy milk; it is dried and sold in sheets. **Dried sweet tofu strips** are chewy and only slightly sweet. They are brown in color and are used in vegetarian cooking as a meat substitute.

seeds. The paste can be quite hard and should be mixed with a little sesame oil or water to make it into a smooth paste. Savory sesame paste should not be confused with the sweet sesame paste that is used in some cakes and desserts. Substitute tahini mixed with sesame oil to give it a more pronounced flavor.

Sichuan peppercorns have a sharp pungency that tingles and slightly numbs the

lips and tongue, an effect known in Chinese as *ma la* "numb hot."

Tamarind is the fruit of the tamarind tree seed pod. The dried pulp is sold in packets or jars and generally still has some seeds and pod fibers mixed in. It is used as a souring agent in many dishes. To obtain tamarind juice, soak the pulp in warm water for 5 minutes, mash well and then strain and discard

the seeds and fibers.

Turmeric root resembles ginger when fresh but is commonly sold in dried form as a yellow powder. Turmeric turns dishes yellow and has a mild flavor. **Ground turmeric** powder is sold in the spice section of supermarkets

Tofu Skin Rolls with Sesame Ginger Dip

4 cups (200 g) fresh
 bean sprouts
1/2 cup (50 g) *enokitaki*
 mushrooms, separated,
 cleaned and blanched
 (see note)
2 carrots, peeled and cut
 into very fine strips
1 cup (110 g) sugar snap
 or snow peas, sliced
 thinly lengthwise
4 sheets dried tofu skin
1 tablespoon flour
2 tablespoons oil

Sesame Ginger Dip
2 tablespoons dark
 sesame paste or tahini,
 blended with 5 tea-
 spoons water
1/2 teaspoon dark soy
 sauce
1/2 teaspoon salt
1 tablespoon sugar
4 teaspoons black
 Chinese vinegar
1 teaspoon sesame oil
2 cloves garlic, minced
1 green onion (scallion),
 thinly sliced
2 slices fresh ginger,
 minced
1 red finger-length chili,
 deseeded and minced

Serves 4
Preparation time: 15 mins
Cooking time: 10 mins

1 Bring a large pot of lightly salted water to a boil
and add the bean sprouts, mushrooms, carrots, and
snow peas. Stir a few times, leave in the water for
about 30 seconds, then transfer to a colander, rinse in
cool water, drain, and set aside.
2 Cut each tofu skin sheet in half. Place one half on
top of the other. Repeat, ending up with 4 layered
rectangles about 8 x 10 in (20 x 25 cm).
3 Place the vegetables in a mixing bowl, sprinkle
evenly with the flour and mix. Divide the vegetables
evenly into 4 portions, and place them neatly at the
edge of each of the 4 rectangles. Roll the skins over
the vegetables to form cylinders. To prevent the tofu
skin from opening up while frying, seal the skin with
a dab of paste made from flour and water.
4 Heat the oil in a large skillet over high heat and
when the oil is hot, but not smoking, gently place
the rolls in the pan and fry for about 2 minutes, then
turn and fry the other side for another 2 minutes.
The skins should turn light golden brown, but be
careful not to scorch them. When done, remove from
the skillet and place on paper towels on a plate to
remove excess oil.
5 When cool, cut each roll at an angle into 3 pieces
and serve with the Sesame Ginger Dip.
6 To make the Sesame Ginger Dip, stir the liquid ingredients together in a mixing bowl until well blended,
then stir in the remaining ingredients and serve.

Enokitaki mushrooms or golden mushrooms are
clusters of slender, cream-colored stalks with tiny caps,
and are sometimes available fresh and canned—the
tough end of the stems must be discarded before use.

Tofu with Ginger and Chinese Mushrooms

Tofu is very popular in Chinese kitchens because it blends well with the strong seasonings and complex flavors in this cuisine and may be combined with virtually any other ingredients. It is also highly nutritious and economical. In this recipe, tofu is combined with dried black Chinese mushroom, dried shrimp, ginger, green onions and savory seasonings to produce a dish that warms the body, stimulates digestion and serenades the palate.

8 oz (250 g) bok choy or cabbage leaves, sliced
$1/3$ cup (90 ml) + 2 tablespoons oil
2 cakes firm tofu (10 oz/300 g each), drained, halved then quartered to yield 16 pieces
2 slices ginger, finely sliced
1 green onion (scallion), cut into 3 sections
6 large dried black Chinese mushrooms, soaked in hot water for 20 minutes then drained, tough stems discarded
$1/4$ cup (60 ml) water
2 teaspoons cornstarch mixed with 2 tablespoons water

Sauce
2 tablespoons soy sauce
1 teaspoon salt
1 tablespoon sugar
1 tablespoon rice wine
1 teaspoon freshly-ground black pepper
1 tablespoon sesame oil

1 Mix the Sauce ingredients and set aside.
2 Blanch the bok choy or cabbage in boiling water for 1 minute, rinse under cold running water, drain, and set aside.
3 Heat the $1/3$ cup (90 ml) of oil in a wok over high heat until hot but not smoking. Add the tofu pieces and turn gently with a spatula until light golden on all sides. Remove and set on a rack or on paper towels to drain. Discard the oil.
4 Heat the remaining 2 tablespoons of oil in a wok until hot but not smoking. Add the ginger, green onion and mushrooms, and stir-fry for 2 minutes. Then add the tofu and continue to stir-fry for another 1 to 2 minutes.
5 Stir the Sauce, then add to the tofu and stir-fry mixture. For more gravy, add the $1/4$ cup (60 ml) of water. Add the cornstarch mixture, stir to blend, cover and reduce the heat to medium. Cook for 6 minutes.
6 Separate the bok choy or cabbage leaves and line the edges of a serving dish with them. Transfer the braised tofu onto the dish and serve.

Serves 4
Preparation time: **15 mins**
Cooking time: **20 mins**

Stir-fried Tofu with Roasted Peanuts and Black Bean Paste

This is a tasty, lively dish with firm and crunchy textures and plenty of spice. It goes well with rice, and could also be used as a stuffing for various wraps, such as Chinese pancakes, seaweed sheets, or whole leaves of iceberg lettuce.

2 tablespoons oil

1–2 red finger-length chilies, halved lengthwise, deseeded, and minced

3 cloves garlic, minced

2 slices fresh ginger, minced

1 green onion (scallion), minced

$^1/_2$ head cabbage, cut into squares

2 cakes pressed tofu (*tau kwa*), about 10 oz/300 g cubed (see note)

$^1/_3$ cup (65 g) roasted peanuts, shells and skins removed

1 stalk celery, tough fibers removed, diced

Sauce

2 tablespoons black bean paste (see note)

2 teaspoons sugar

2 teaspoons rice wine

1 tablespoon water

1 Combine the Sauce ingredients in a bowl and set aside.

2 Heat the oil in a wok over high heat until very hot, and stir-fry the chili, garlic, ginger, and green onion. Add the cabbage and tofu. Stir-fry for 1 minute.

3 Add the Sauce and continue to cook for 4 to 5 minutes.

4 Add the peanuts, stir-fry for 30 seconds more or until the peanuts are heated through, and remove from the heat. Place in a serving dish, garnish with the diced celery, and serve.

Black bean paste is made from fermented soybeans, and is an important seasoning in Asian dishes. It has a strong, salty flavor and is available from Asian food stores.

Pressed tofu is a variety of firm tofu with most of the moisture pressed out of it. It usually comes in the form of a small, firm rectangular block and is bright yellow. Substitute with firm tofu if unavailable.

Serves 4
Preparation time: **20 mins**
Cooking time: **10 mins**

Tofu Steaks with Chili Paste

Tofu has long been popular as a meat substitute in China, and has made a big impact in the West, especially when cooked with robust seasonings and fragrant sauces, in order to become palatable and earn its place on the dining table. You may use black bean paste instead of chili sauce and try dusting the cooked steaks with Sichuan pepper-salt for a different taste. This recipe transforms tofu into a "steak" that satisfies as much as any filet mignon—and it's even easier to prepare.

2 cakes firm tofu
  (10 oz/300 g each)
4 tablespoons oil
4 cloves garlic, minced
1 tablespoon chili paste
2 green onion (scallions),
  cut into sections

Sauce
1 tablespoon soy sauce
1 tablespoon rice wine
1 teaspoon sesame oil
1 teaspoon sugar
Salt and freshly-ground
  black pepper to taste

Serves 4
Preparation time: 10 mins
Cooking time: 10 mins

1 Halve the tofu cakes horizontally to form 4 pieces. Gently press the tofu with paper towels to remove excess moisture. Set aside.

2 Combine all the Sauce ingredients and set aside.

3 Heat the oil in a skillet over high heat until hot but not smoking. Place the tofu in the skillet, and shake the pan gently to prevent sticking. Cook for 2 to 3 minutes, turn carefully with a spatula, and cook the other side for 2 to 3 minutes.

4 Push the tofu steaks to the side of the skillet. Add the garlic and chili paste, stir to blend the flavors and prevent sticking.

5 Add the Sauce, shake the skillet well to mix all the ingredients, cover with lid, reduce the heat to low and cook for 2 minutes. Add the green onions, turn the tofu over, and cook for another 2 minutes. Transfer to a serving dish and season with a little salt and pepper.

Fried Tofu with Sweet Hoisin Sauce

This recipe employs a traditional Sichuan cooking technique called *gan bian* ("crinkle-fry"), in which the main ingredient is continuously stir-fried in a small amount of oil over medium heat until it starts to "crinkle," such as in the famous Sichuan dish, "crinkle-fried green beans."

3 tablespoons oil
1 teaspoon salt
10 oz (300 g) dried sweet tofu strips, cut into strips (about 3 cups), see note
1 carrot, peeled and coarsely grated
1 teaspoon black Chinese vinegar
1 teaspoon sesame oil
$1/2$ cup (20 g) Chinese celery leaves or coriander leaves (cilantro), coarsely chopped

Sauce
3 teaspoons hoisin sauce
1 teaspoon sugar
3 teaspoons rice wine
2 teaspoons soy sauce

Serves 4
Preparation time: **10 mins**
Cooking time: **25 mins**

1 Heat the oil in a wok until hot, but not smoking. Add in the salt, and stir in the dried sweet tofu strips. Stir-fry continuously over medium heat until the tofu strips start to crinkle and turn crispy, about 15 minutes. Remove and set aside on a plate.

2 In the remaining oil, stir-fry the carrot for 30 seconds, then add the Sauce ingredients. Cook for another minute, then add the fried tofu strips. Stir-fry for 1 minute, ensuring that the tofu strips are coated with the Sauce. Add the vinegar and stir-fry for 30 seconds more. Turn off the heat, add the sesame oil, and toss to combine.

3 Transfer to a serving plate, garnish with the chopped celery leaves or coriander leaves, and serve.

Dried sweet tofu strips, or tau kee (also known as *teem chok*) are brown in color. These slightly sweetened hard dried tofu strips are often used in vegetarian cuisine as a meat substitute. If you cannot find them, use pressed or dried tofu instead.

Stir-fried Tofu with Vegetables

2 tablespoons oil
3 slices fresh ginger, minced
2 cloves garlic, minced
$1/2$ cup (125) ml water
2 cakes firm tofu (about 10 oz/300 g each), cubed
1 cup (160 g) fresh or frozen mixed vegetables, such as peas, corn, diced carrots
6 dried black Chinese mushrooms, soaked in warm water for 20 minutes, stems discarded and caps sliced
1 teaspoon ground Sichuan pepper
$1/2$ teaspoon freshly-ground black pepper
1 teaspoon cornstarch mixed with 1 tablespoon water
1 green onion (scallion), minced
1 red finger-length chili, thinly sliced
1 teaspoon sesame oil

Sauce
1 tablespoon hoisin sauce
$1/2$ teaspoon sugar
1 teaspoon soy sauce
2 teaspoons rice wine

1 Combine the Sauce ingredients in a bowl and set aside.
2 Heat the oil in a wok over high heat until smoking and add the minced ginger and garlic. Stir-fry for 10 seconds.
3 Add the Sauce, stir a few times, add the water, and stir again to blend. When the Sauce comes to a boil, add the tofu, vegetables and mushrooms and stir-fry. Cover, reduce the heat to medium, and cook for 7 to 8 minutes.
4 Add the Sichuan pepper and black pepper, stirring to blend. Cover and simmer 1 more minute before adding the cornstarch mixture. Stir until the Sauce thickens and bring to a boil again.
5 Remove from the heat, stir in the green onion, chili, and sesame oil, and serve with rice.

Serves 4
Preparation time: 5 mins
Cooking time: 15 mins

Steamed Tofu with Black Mushrooms

1 cake soft tofu (about 10 oz/300 g)

5 dried black Chinese mushrooms, soaked in warm water for 20 minutes, stems discarded and caps sliced

3 pieces dried wood ear fungus, soaked in hot water for 20 minutes and minced (see note)

5 cloves garlic, minced

5 slices fresh ginger, minced

6 green onions (scallions), minced

Chopped celery leaves or fresh coriander leaves (cilantro) to garnish

Seasonings

1 teaspoon salt
1 teaspoon sugar
1 teaspoon soy sauce
1 tablespoon rice wine
$1/2$ teaspoon freshly-ground black pepper
2 tablespoons sesame oil

1 Heat the water in a steamer pot with rack and bring to a boil.

2 Meanwhile, wash the tofu, drain well, and pat dry with paper towels (or let the tofu drain on a rack for one hour before preparation). Using your fingers, crumble and mash the tofu into one medium heat-proof bowl or four individual serving bowls (as shown).

3 Stir the Seasonings into the mashed tofu. Add the diced mushrooms, wood ear fungus, garlic, ginger, and green onions. Stir until evenly blended.

4 Set the bowl(s) of tofu mixture on the steaming rack, cover the steamer tightly, and steam for 20 minutes. Remove the bowl(s) from the steamer, set onto a plate, and garnish with the chopped celery leaves or fresh coriander leaves before serving.

Wood ear fungus is a type of thin, crinkly mushroom added to dishes for its crunchy texture. It is available both fresh and dried. Wash well and discard any hard patch in the center. Soak dried wook ear fungus in water until soft before using.

Serves 4
Preparation time: 20 mins
Cooking time: 25 mins

Braised Tofu with Vegetables

For best results, prepare this dish in a traditional Chinese claypot, which is designed to allow all the seasoning flavors to blend slowly and completely. A normal casserole pot can also be used, however.

4 cups (1 liter) water
Two 8-in (20-cm) pieces
  dried *konbu* seaweed
  (optional, see note)
2 teaspoons rice wine
1 cake soft tofu (about
  10 oz/300 g each),
  cubed
1 daikon radish, peeled,
  cut lengthwise and
  sliced thinly at an angle
1 carrot, cut lengthwise
  and sliced thinly
6 button mushrooms,
  wiped clean and cut
  into 3 pieces each
1 small cooked bamboo
  shoot, washed, drained,
  and thinly sliced (see
  note)
1 onion, peeled and cut
  into thin crescents
1 teaspoon sugar
2 teaspoons salt
2 teaspoons soy sauce
20 fresh snow peas, tops,
  tails, and ribs removed
1 red finger-length chili,
  halved lengthwise
2 teaspoons sesame oil

1 Put the water, *konbu* (if using), and rice wine into a claypot or casserole dish. Bring to a boil, reduce the heat to low, cover, and cook for 20 minutes.
2 Add the tofu, daikon radish, carrot, mushrooms, bamboo shoot and onions. Stir in the sugar, salt, and soy sauce, cover, and cook for another 10 minutes.
3 Add the snow peas and chilies, cooking for 1 more minute. Remove from the heat.
4 Drizzle in the sesame oil, mixing well, and serve.

Bamboo shoots are the fresh shoots of the bamboo plant. Pre-cooked bamboo shoots, packed in water, can be found in the refrigerated section of supermarkets. Canned bamboo shoots are also pre-cooked but should be boiled for 5 minutes to refresh before using.

Konbu or dried kelp is a type of seaweed commonly used in Japanese cooking. It has a dark brown color, often with whitish patches of salt, and is sold in strips or small folded sheets. Look for konbu in the Japanese section of supermarkets.

Serves 4
Preparation time: **30 mins**
Cooking time: **45 mins**

Stuffed Tofu with Sweet Chili Sauce Dip

An alternative presentation of this dish is to dice the deep-fried tofu, arrange it on a plate, and scatter with the shredded vegetables and bean sprouts.

4 cakes firm tofu
  (10 oz/300 g each)
1/2 teaspoon salt
1 cup (250 ml) oil
1 cup (50 g) bean sprouts
1/2 cup (90 g) finely
  shredded jicama or
  carrot
1/2 cup (60 g) finely
  shredded cucumber

Sweet Chili Sauce Dip
2 red finger-length chilies,
  deseeded
1 clove garlic, peeled
1/4 teaspoon salt
1 tablespoon sugar
1 1/2 tablespoons water
1 tablespoon vinegar
1 tablespoon tomato
  ketchup

Serves 4
Preparation time: **20 mins**
Cooking time: **15 mins**

1 Halve each piece of tofu diagonally. Dab gently with paper towels to absorb excess moisture. Sprinkle the salt over the tofu and set aside.

2 To make the Sweet Chili Sauce Dip, grind the chilies, garlic, salt and sugar in a blender. Add the water, vinegar and tomato ketchup, and grind to make a smooth sauce. Place into a serving bowl.

3 Heat the oil in a wok over medium heat and gently lower half of the tofu pieces into the oil. Fry until crisp and golden brown, about 4 minutes. Remove from the oil and drain on paper towels. Repeat with the remaining tofu. When cool enough to handle, make a horizontal slit into the side of each piece of tofu to create a pocket, taking care not to cut through the tofu (see photo). Set aside.

4 Blanch the bean sprouts in a pan of boiling water for 10 seconds. Then drain and refresh under cold running water. Toss the bean sprouts, jicama (or carrot) and cucumber together in a bowl.

5 Stuff each tofu pocket with the mixed vegetables.

Make a horizontal slit into the side of each piece of deep-fried tofu.

Stuff each tofu pocket with the bean sprouts, jicama (or carrot) and cucumber.

Grilled Eggplant with Tofu and Lemon Soy Dressing

1 cake firm tofu
  (10 oz/300 g each)
$^1/_2$ teaspoon salt
1 cup (250 ml) oil
3 Asian eggplants (about
  1 lb/500 g)
1 small onion, thinly
  sliced
1 red finger-length chili,
  coarsely chopped
  (optional)

Lemon Soy Dressing
1 tablespoon freshly
  squeezed lime or
  lemon juice
2 teaspoons soy sauce
1 teaspoon sugar

1 Sprinkle both sides of the tofu with the salt. Heat the oil in a wok or saucepan and deep-fry the tofu until golden brown on both sides. Drain on paper towels and cut into cubes. Cool to room temperature and set aside.

2 Score the eggplant lengthwise with the tip of a knife. Grill or broil until soft, about 10 minutes. When cool enough to handle, peel the eggplants and cut into 2-in (5-cm) long pieces. Arrange the slices on a serving platter.

3 Combine the Lemon Soy Dressing ingredients and pour over the eggplants before serving. Garnish with the onion, chilies, and fried tofu cubes.

Serves 4
Preparation time: **15 mins**
Cooking time: **10 mins**

Thai-style Tofu with Mushrooms

10 fresh button mushrooms
2 cakes firm tofu (10 oz/300 g each), diced
1/4 cup (60 ml) freshly squeezed lime
2 tablespoons fish sauce
1/2 teaspoon salt
1/2 teaspoon sugar

3 tablespoons Roasted Rice Powder (see note)
1 red finger-length chili, deseeded and minced
1 green onion (scallion), minced
2 shallots, thinly sliced
2 tablespoons fresh

coriander leaves (cilantro), chopped
1/2 cup (20 g) mint leaves, chopped

Serves 4 to 6
Preparation time: **10 mins**
Cooking time: **10 mins**

1 Steam the mushrooms for 5 minutes and slice.

2 Combine the tofu with the mushrooms in a bowl. Mix the lime juice, fish sauce, salt and sugar, and stir into the tofu and mushrooms. Stir in the Roasted Rice Powder, chilies, green onion, shallots, coriander, and mint leaves.

3 Arrange the tofu mixture on a serving platter, surround with vegetables such as lettuce leaves, cabbage leaves, sliced cucumbers, and green beans, as desired.

To make **Roasted Rice Powder**, dry-roast 1/2 cup (120 g) uncooked Thai jasmine or long-grain rice in a skillet over medium heat, stirring constantly until light brown, then grind to a fine powder in a food processor. Store in an airtight container.

Stir-fried Vegetarian Rice Noodles

Rice vermicelli is a popular alternative to wheat noodles in vegetarian cooking, and is an excellent choice for those who do not tolerate wheat products well.

8 dried black Chinese mushrooms, soaked in hot water for 20 minutes
1 teaspoon salt
7 oz (200 g) dried rice vermicelli (*beehoon* or *mifen*)
1 tablespoon sesame oil
2 tablespoons oil
$1/2$ in (1 cm) fresh ginger, cut into fine shreds
2 cloves garlic, minced
1 teaspoon soy sauce
1 teaspoon sugar
$1/2$ teaspoon salt
$1^1/_2$ cups (200 g) thinly sliced cabbage
1 small carrot, cut into fine strips
1 bunch garlic chives, snipped into lengths
1 tablespoon vegetarian mushroom oyster sauce (see note)
1 cup (50 g) bean sprouts, washed and trimmed
1 teaspoon freshly-ground black pepper
1 red finger-length chili, sliced, to garnish
2 limes, cut in wedges

1 After soaking the mushrooms, remove and discard the stems and slice the caps, reserving the soaking liquid. Set the mushrooms aside.
2 Bring a pot of water with the salt to a full boil, and add the rice vermicelli. Cook for exactly 3 minutes, then drain. Place the rice vermicelli in a mixing bowl and drizzle with the sesame oil; toss to coat thoroughly and set aside.
3 Heat the oil in a wok until smoking, and add the ginger, garlic, and mushrooms and stir-fry 1 to 2 minutes. Add the soy sauce, sugar, and salt, and stir-fry.
4 Add the cabbage and carrot and stir-fry for 2 to 3 minutes; stir in 3 tablespoons of the reserved mushroom water and cook for 2 to 3 minutes more.
5 Add the garlic chives and vegetarian mushroom oyster sauce and stir-fry for 2 minutes, then add the bean sprouts and stir-fry for 1 more minute.
6 Add the black pepper, stir to distribute evenly, and place the vegetables on the rice vermicelli. Toss to combine, garnish with the sliced chili, and serve with slices of lime.

Vegetarian mushroom oyster sauce is a soy-based sauce that is the vegetarian substitute for regular oyster sauce.

Serves 4
Preparation time: 15 mins + 20 mins soaking time
Cooking time: 30 mins

Tossed Noodles with Peppers, Sprouts and Sesame Garlic Dressing

This traditional and very tasty form of Chinese "fast food" is quick and easy to prepare. You may apply the recipe to virtually any type of noodle, adjust the sauce to your own taste, and add whatever sort of vegetables you like best. Works great as a salad or appetizer!

1 teaspoon salt
8 oz (250 g) dried wheat noodles or fettucini
1 cup (50 g) fresh bean sprouts, washed and drained
1 bell pepper, deseeded and cut into strips
2 green onions (scallions), minced
Freshly-ground black pepper to taste

Sesame Garlic Dressing
2 tablespoons dark sesame paste or tahini, blended with 3 teaspoons water
1 teaspoon black Chinese vinegar
$1/2$ teaspoon salt
$1 1/2$ teaspoons sugar
1 teaspoon vegetarian mushroom oyster sauce (see note)
1 teaspoon soy sauce
1 tablespoon olive oil
2 cloves garlic, minced

1 In a large mixing bowl, stir together the Sesame Garlic Dressing ingredients, then set aside.
2 Bring a large pot of water with the salt to a boil, and cook the noodles according to the package directions.
3 Drain the noodles, rinse under cool water, and drain again. Place the noodles in a large bowl. Add the Sesame Garlic Dressing and mix well. Toss in the bean sprouts and red bell pepper. Garnish with the green onions and ground black pepper.

Vegetarian mushroom oyster sauce is a soy-based sauce that is the vegetarian substitute for regular oyster sauce.

Serves 4
Preparation time: 10 mins
Cooking time: 8 mins

Noodles with Sesame Soy Dressing

In addition to its delicious taste, this dish delivers a rich parcel of nutritional and medicinal benefits. The sauce contains sesame paste, which is an excellent source of essential fatty acids and benefits bowel functions. Ground peanuts, known in ancient China as "the food of the immortals", provide a quick source of energy, and Sichuan pepper assists digestion and assimilation of nutrients. The recipe below uses ordinary dried wheat noodles that may be purchased in any Asian grocery, but you may also use fresh noodles, as well as rice, buckwheat, egg, or any other type of noodle you wish.

10 oz (300 g) dried wheat noodles or fettucini
1 teaspoon sesame oil
1 tablespoon coarsely ground roasted peanuts
2 green onions (scallions), finely sliced

Sesame Soy Dressing
3 teaspoons dark sesame paste or tahini
$2/3$ cup (165 ml) water
3 teaspoons dark soy sauce
1 teaspoon sugar
$1/2$ teaspoon ground Sichuan pepper or freshly-ground black pepper
2 teaspoons red chili oil
1 teaspoon vinegar

Serves 4
Preparation time: 5 mins
Cooking time: 5 mins

1 To mix the Sesame Soy Dressing, place the sesame paste in the bottom of a bowl and slowly pour in the water whilst whisking continuously to blend. Add the soy sauce, sugar and Sichuan pepper, while stirring continuously, then add the chili oil and the vinegar, and blend well.

2 Bring a large pot of water to a boil, add the dried noodles and cook according to the directions on the package.

3 Drain the noodles in a colander, rinse in cold water, drain, place in a large bowl, then drizzle on 1 teaspoon sesame oil and mix well.

4 Add the Sesame Soy Dressing to the noodles and toss to mix well, then sprinkle on the ground peanuts and chopped spring onions.

5 Serve in a large serving dish at the table, or distribute equally into individual noodle bowls and serve.

While almost any sort of noodle may be used here, the best choice for both taste and nutrition are freshly made noodles, either from your local market or hand-made in your own kitchen. And if you like the tangy flavor of fresh coriander leaves, it makes a most palatable garnish for this dish. The possibilities are virtually endless!

Vegetable and Mushroom Noodle Soup

This recipe may also be prepared with any sort of leafy vegetables, as well as various types of noodles—for example, it's excellent with rice or mung bean vermicelli. Simply follow the label directions for preparing the noodles, then add to the soup.

5 dried black Chinese mushrooms, soaked in warm water for 20 minutes, stems discarded and caps sliced

6 cups (1$^1/_2$ liters) vegetable stock or water

1 tablespoon Chinese wolfberries (see note—optional)

2 teaspoons salt

2 teaspoons soy sauce

1 teaspoon sugar

1 cup (125 g) fresh lotus root, thinly sliced (optional)

$^3/_4$ cup (150 g) bamboo shoots, blanched and drained, halved lengthwise and thinly sliced (see note)

7 oz (200 g) dried wheat noodles or fettucini

1 cup (125 g) sliced bok choy or cabbage leaves

2 teaspoons sesame oil

Serves 4
Preparation time: 10 mins
+ 20 mins soaking time
Cooking time: 40 mins

1 Drain the soaked mushrooms, cut them in half, and reserve the soaking liquid. Set aside.

2 Bring the vegetable stock or water to a boil in a large pot. Add the wolfberry, if using and mushrooms, cover, and cook for 1 to 2 minutes.

3 Add the salt, soy sauce, and sugar, then add the lotus root and bamboo shoots. Cover, reduce the heat to low, and cook for 3 to 4 minutes. Remove from the heat and set aside, covered.

4 Bring a large pot of water to a boil, and cook the noodles according to the package directions.

5 Remove and drain the noodles, rinse under cool water, then drain and divide the noodles into 4 individual serving bowls.

6 Bring the soup to a boil, add the bok choy and remove from the heat. Stir in the sesame oil, and ladle the soup and vegetables over the noodles.

Chinese wolfberries, also known as Chinese boxthorns or matrimony vines, are available from Chinese medicine or grocery stores. Dried cranberries or other small, taut berries may be substituted.

Bamboo shoots, are the fresh shoots of the bamboo plant. Pre-cooked bamboo shoots, packed in water, can be found in the refrigerated section of supermarkets. Canned bamboo shoots are also pre-cooked but should be boiled for 5 minutes to refresh before using.

Stir-fried Vegetarian Brown Rice

Many of the ingredients in this version of the ubiquitous fried rice, such as black Chinese mushrooms, may have possible medicinal properties. You may also try other combinations of vegetables, such as corn, turnips, and other types of mushrooms.

1 cup (220 g) uncooked brown rice, rinsed and drained
2¹/₂ cups (625 ml) vegetable soup stock
2 tablespoons oil
2 onions, thinly sliced
4 cloves garlic, minced
1 carrot, halved lengthwise, and sliced thinly
1 bell pepper, deseeded and diced
6 dried black Chinese mushrooms, soaked for 20 minutes and drained, caps diced
¹/₂ cup (80 g) fresh or frozen green peas
Fresh coriander leaves (cilantro), to garnish

Seasonings
¹/₂ teaspoon salt
1 teaspoon sugar
2 teaspoons soy sauce
1 teaspoon freshly-ground black pepper

1 Place the drained rice and vegetable stock in a saucepan, bring to a boil over medium heat, and cook until the rice is tender, about 25 minutes. Allow the rice to cool completely.
2 Heat the oil in a wok or large skillet until hot, then add the onion and garlic. Stir-fry for 1 minute. Add the carrots, bell pepper, mushrooms, peas, and Seasonings. Continue to stir-fry for 2–3 minutes, then add the cooked rice. Mix well and cook until the rice is heated through, about 5 minutes. Adjust the Seasonings with more salt and soy sauce as desired.
3 Remove from the heat, and transfer the rice and vegetables to a serving bowl.

Serves 4
Preparation time: 20 mins + overnight soaking
Cooking time: 1 hour

Healthy Rice and Soybeans

You may use this extremely healthy and tasty rice-and-beans combo as the staple dish to be eaten with other main dishes.

$^1/_2$ cup (100 g) dried soy-beans (see note)
3 cups (750 ml) water
$^1/_2$ teaspoon salt
1 cup (220 g) uncooked brown rice, washed and soaked in 2 cups (500 ml) water

Garnishes
1 carrot, diced and blanched
1 cup minced bell pepper
1 bunch coriander leaves (cilantro), finely chopped
2 green onions (scallions), finely chopped
Freshly-ground black (or Sichuan) pepper, to taste

1 Clean and rinse the soybeans well. Drain and place in a saucepan with water to cover by at least 1 in ($2^1/_2$ cm). Soak overnight.

2 The next day, drain the water from the soybeans and add 3 cups of fresh water. Bring to a boil over medium heat, cover, and reduce the heat to low. Cook until the beans absorb all the water, about $1^1/_2$ hours. Check the beans occasionally to make sure they don't scorch. When soft, transfer them to a bowl and set aside to cool.

3 Add the salt to the soaked rice and bring to a full boil. Cover, reduce the heat to very low, and cook for about 30 minutes, or until the rice starts to crackle. Do not remove the lid while cooking. Remove from the heat and set aside, still covered, for 15 minutes. Transfer to a bowl and set aside to cool, turning the rice once or twice with a spoon to cool and dry evenly.

4 When the rice and beans have cooled to warm, carefully fold them together in a large serving bowl. Stir in all or any of the Garnishes and serve.

Soybeans are an abundant source of high quality vegetable protein and oil, and contain virtually no cholesterol. They are a rich source of vitamin B, minerals and fiber.

Serves 4
Preparation time: overnight soaking
Cooking time: 50 mins

Tomato and Cashew Rice Pilau

2 tablespoons ghee or oil
2 cinnamon sticks
5 cloves
5 cardamom pods
2 onions, finely sliced
3 green finger-length chilies, deseeded and slit lengthwise
2 tablespoons ginger paste (see note)
2 tablespoons garlic paste (see note)
3 tablespoons chopped coriander leaves (cilantro),
3 tablespoons chopped mint leaves
2$^1/_2$ cups (500 g) uncooked basmati rice, washed and drained (see note)
1 can (12 oz/350 g) peeled chopped tomatoes
1 cup (250 ml) thick coconut milk
1 teaspoon ground turmeric
1$^1/_2$ teaspoons salt
2$^1/_2$ cups (625 ml) water
$^1/_4$ cup (40 g) raisins
$^2/_3$ cup (80 g) fried or roasted cashew nuts

1 Heat the ghee or oil in a pot over medium heat. Stir-fry the whole spices—cinnamon, cloves and cardamom—and the onion, green chilies, ginger and garlic pastes until the onion is golden brown, about 10 minutes.

2 Add the coriander and mint leaves, then stir in the rice and mix well. Add the remaining ingredients except the raisins and cashew nuts and mix thoroughly.

3 Cover with a tight fitting lid, reduce the heat to low, and cook for 15 to 20 minutes. Alternatively, transfer the mixture to an electric rice cooker and cook according to the manufacturer's instructions. Stir occasionally until the rice is cooked and all the moisture has been absorbed. Fluff the rice up and mix in the raisins and cashew nuts just before serving.

Basmati rice is an Indian long-grain rice variety characterised by its thinness and fragrance. The grains stay whole and separate when cooked with oil and spices. Substitute long-grain Thai jasmine rice.

Garlic or ginger paste can be prepared by blending or pounding the required amount of garlic or ginger needed with some water. A garlic press may also be used. Since these pastes are used in many of the recipes in this book, you may prefer to make a large batch in advance it in the refrigerator.

Serves 4–6
Preparation time: **15 mins**
Cooking time: **25 mins**

Red Rice with Coconut

1 cup (200 g) uncooked glutinous rice
1 cup (200 g) uncooked red or brown rice
2 drops pandanus essence
1 cup (250 ml) thick coconut milk
$1^1/_2$ teaspoons salt
$^1/_4$ teaspoon fenugreek seeds
$^3/_4$ in (2 cm) fresh ginger, peeled and thinly sliced
3 shallots, thinly sliced

1 Soak the rice for 4 hours or overnight. Drain and wash the rice in several rinses of water until the water runs clear. Place the rice in a large bowl with enough water to cover it, about $3^1/_2$ in (8 cm) above the rice.
2 Line a regular stainless steel steamer or a bamboo steamer with a muslin cloth. Spoon the rice onto the cloth and spread evenly. Steam, covered, over rapidly boiling water for 30 minutes.
3 Combine the coconut milk and salt in a large bowl. Add the pandanus essence to the coconut milk and mix well. Add the steamed rice and stir with a wooden spoon until all the coconut milk has been absorbed by the rice. Add the fenugreek seeds, ginger and shallots, and mix well.
4 Steam the rice mixture, as in step 2, for another 30 minutes. Serve immediately.

Pandanus essence, also known as pandanus extract, is a delightful scent that's used throughout Southeast Asia to flavor dishes and desserts. To make pandanus essence, blend 10 pandanus leaves with 1 cup (250 ml) water in a blender or food processor and strain the liquid. Only a few drops are needed. Bottled pandanus essence is available in Asian food stores.

Serves 4
Preparation time: **15 mins**
Cooking time: **40 mins**

Vegetarian Sandwich with Sesame Spread

This modern adaptation of a sort of "Chinese sandwich" calls for a high-quality whole-grain bread, thinly sliced and toasted.

3 slices whole-grain
   bread, toasted
1 tomato, thinly sliced
12 to 15 celery leaves,
   coarsely chopped
2 to 3 leaves lettuce
1 onion, thinly sliced

Sesame Spread

$1/4$ cup (35 g) raw sun-
   flower seeds, presoaked
   3 hours in cool water
   and drained
2 tablespoons dark
   sesame paste or tahini,
   blended with 3 tea-
   spoons water
$1/2$ tablespoon sesame oil
$1/4$ teaspoon salt
$1/2$ teaspoon sugar
1 teaspoon soy sauce
1 teaspoon freshly-
   ground black pepper
Garlic to taste, roasted
   (optional)

1 To prepare the Sesame Spread, place all the ingredients in a blender, and blend until smooth. Adjust seasonings, if necessary.

2 To assemble the sandwich, place a slice of toast on a plate and cover with one-quarter of the Sesame Spread. Arrange half of the tomato slices, chopped celery leaves, lettuce and onion slices on top of the spread. Top with a second slice of toast spread-side down, then cover the top of that slice with Sesame Spread and arrange the remaining vegetables on it. Complete the sandwich with the third slice of toast placed spread-side down.

3 Cut in half with sharp knife, or serve whole.

Serves 1
Preparation time: **10 mins**
Assembling time: **5 mins**

Bean Sprouts with Sesame Garlic Dressing

Most Chinese salads are made with vegetables that have been lightly blanched, and the range of ingredients used for salads in Chinese cuisine is much broader than those in the West. The actual word for salad courses in Chinese is *leng pan*, which simply means "cold dish." This could refer to platters of cold cuts, tofu, beans, and anything else served cold. This recipe calls for two types of sprouts. Either one of the sprouts or both taste as good.

4 oz (125 g) fresh soy bean sprouts, rinsed
4 oz (125 g) fresh mung bean sprouts, rinsed
1 teaspoon salt
2 green onions (scallions), finely chopped (optional)

Sesame Garlic Dressing
2 to 3 cloves garlic, minced
2 tablespoons soy sauce
1 tablespoon sesame oil
1 teaspoon sugar
$^1/_2$ teaspoon salt
$^1/_2$ teaspoon freshly-ground black pepper
1 teaspoon vinegar

1 To make the Sesame Garlic Dressing, combine all the ingredients in a small bowl and set aside.
2 Bring a large pot of water to a rolling boil and add 1 teaspoon salt.
3 Blanch the soy bean sprouts and the mung bean sprouts in the boiling water very briefly (about 5 seconds). Remove from the pot and let it drain in a colander.
4 Run the blanched bean sprouts under cold running water (5 seconds). Let it drain in a colander and set aside.
5 Mix the two kinds of sprouts together in a bowl, then add the Sesame Garlic Dressing and toss well. Garnish with the chopped green onions, if using.

Serves 4
Preparation time: **10 mins**
Cooking time: **5 mins**

Mixed Vegetable Salad with Sweet and Spicy Peanut Dressing

1 cake firm tofu
(10 oz/300 g)
$^1/_2$ teaspoon salt
1 cup (250 ml) oil
1 cucumber, peeled and sliced
$1^1/_2$ cups (200 g) thinly sliced cabbage,
10 lettuce leaves, sliced or torn
2 potatoes, boiled, peeled, and cubed
3 hard-boiled eggs, peeled and sliced
Deep-fried melinjo nut wafers (*krupuk emping*, see note) or shrimp crackers (optional)

Peanut Dressing
1 tablespoon tamarind pulp soaked in $^1/_4$ cup (60 ml) warm water, mashed and strained to obtain juice
$1^2/_3$ cups (250 g) raw peanuts, dry roasted, skins removed
2–3 red finger-length chilies
1 in ($2^1/_2$ cm) fresh galangal root
4 cloves garlic
3 kaffir lime leaves
2 teaspoons salt
$^1/_2$ cup (90 g) palm sugar
2 cups (500 ml) hot water

1 Sprinkle both sides of the tofu with the salt. Heat the oil in a wok or saucepan and deep-fry the tofu until golden brown on both sides. Drain on paper towels and cut into 1 in ($2^1/_2$ cm) cubes. Set aside to cool.
2 To prepare the Peanut Dressing, grind the peanuts coarsely in a food processor, then remove and set aside. Grind the chilies, galangal, garlic, kaffir lime leaves, tamarind juice, salt and palm sugar in a spice grinder or blender to form a smooth paste. Add the ground peanuts to the spice paste and pulse a few times. Add the water and pulse to make a thick sauce.
3 Put the tofu, cucumber, cabbage, lettuce and potatoes in a large bowl. Add the Peanut Dressing and toss to mix well. Transfer to a serving platter and top with the sliced egg and melinjo nut wafers.

Melinjo or *belinjo* is the fruit of a tree found in Southeast Asia (particularly Indonesia). Consisting of little but skin and a large seed (nut) inside, the seeds are ground or flattened into wafers, then dried and deep-fried as *emping* crackers (*kerupuk*). The crackers have a slightly bitter taste and are frequently served as a snack or accompaniment to Indonesian dishes.

Serves 4
Preparation time: **15 mins**
Cooking time: **30 mins**

Mixed Salad with Spicy Coconut Dressing

5 cups (250 g) fresh bean sprouts, washed and drained, tails removed,
1 cup (100 g) sliced green beans
$1^1/_2$ cups (150 g) thinly sliced cabbage
$1^1/_2$ cups (150 g) green leafy vegetables such as bok choy or *choy sum* (see note)
$1^1/_2$ cups (150 g) water spinach or regular spinach, tough stems discarded, carefully washed and snipped into sections (see note)

Coconut Dressing
2-3 red finger-length chilies, sliced
3 cloves garlic, peeled
$3/_4$ in (2 cm) fresh galangal root, peeled and sliced
$1/_2$ teaspoon ground coriander
3 kaffir lime leaves, sliced, or 1 teaspoon finely grated lime rind
1 tablespoon shaved palm sugar
1 teaspoon salt
2 cups (200 g) grated fresh coconut

1 Grind all the Coconut Dressing ingredients except the coconut in a food processor or blender. Transfer to a heatproof bowl and stir in the coconut. Place the bowl in a steamer, cover and steam for 30 minutes. Transfer to another bowl and set aside to cool.
2 Blanch the vegetables separately. Drain all the vegetables and place them in a large serving bowl. Add the Coconut Dressing and toss. Serve at room temperature.

Choy sum (*chye sim*), also known as Chinese flowering cabbage, is a leafy green vegetable with crisp crunchy stems. Available in supermarkets in Asia, it is now increasingly available in Western countries too. Substitute any other leafy greens.

Water spinach, also known as water convolvulus or morning glory, is a leafy green vegetable with crunchy, hollow stems. It is commonly used in Southeast Asian and Chinese cooking. It must be washed thoroughly to remove dirt and sand, and the thick, tough ends of stems removed. If unavailable, substitute normal spinach.

If you cannot obtain fresh or frozen grated coconut, use half the amount of dried unsweetened coconut flakes, moistened with a bit of warm water to soften.

Serves 4
Preparation time: 20 mins
Cooking time: 45 mins

Fresh Cucumber Salad with Garlic and Sesame Soy Dressing

10 oz (300 g) baby cucumbers or gherkins
3 to 4 cloves garlic, peeled and crushed

Sesame Soy Dressing
2 tablespoons soy sauce
1 tablespoon sesame oil
1 teaspoon vinegar
1 teaspoon sugar
$^1/_2$ teaspoon salt
$^1/_2$ teaspoon freshly-ground black pepper

1 Wash the cucumbers well, pat dry and place on a cutting board. Use the side of a cleaver or a large knife to press on the cucumbers so they crack open, then cut into 1-in (2$^1/_2$-cm) sections. Place in a large bowl and add the garlic.

2 Combine the Sesame Soy Dressing ingredients and drizzle evenly over the cucumbers and garlic. Toss well to blend the flavors.

3 Cover with plastic wrap and let it marinate in the refrigerator for 1 to 2 hours, or for 30 minutes at room temperature. Transfer to a smaller bowl and serve.

Serves 4
Preparation time: **10 mins**
Assembling time: **2 mins**

Eggplant with Garlic Soy Dressing

4 Asian eggplants (about
   1¹/₂ lbs/700 g)
Fresh coriander leaves
   (cilantro)

Garlic Soy Dressing
6 cloves fresh garlic,
   finely minced
1 teaspoon soy sauce
2 teaspoons black
   Chinese vinegar
¹/₂ teaspoon salt
1 teaspoon sugar
¹/₂ teaspoon freshly-
   ground black pepper
1 tablespoon sesame oil

1 Pierce the eggplants all over with a fork, then cook in a microwave oven on high for 8 minutes, or steam in a steamer for 10 minutes.

2 Drain the eggplants in a colander. When cool enough to handle, cut the eggplants in half lengthwise, then cut each half into sections, and place them in a mixing bowl.

3 Stir all the Garlic Soy Dressing ingredients, except the sesame oil, together in a separate bowl until the sugar and salt are dissolved. Using a whisk or fork, beat in the sesame oil until well blended. Pour the Dressing evenly over the eggplant and toss to coat well. Transfer to a serving dish. Garnish with the coriander leaves.

Serves 4
Preparation time: **10 mins**
Cooking time: **8 mins**

Braised Pumpkin

This is one of the simplest dishes of all to cook, relying entirely on the unadorned rich flavor of pumpkin, which blossoms when allowed to cook in its own juices. Try to select sweet mature pumpkins for this dish. This is a vegetable dish that most children like to eat, which makes it a popular choice for family meals. You may experiment with different flavors, such as adding a cinnamon stick, a sliced vanilla bean or some sliced ginger root to the pot along with the sugar and salt. The finished dish may also be garnished with chopped green onions.

3 tablespoons oil
1 small pumpkin (about 2 lbs/1 kg), peeled and
  deseeded, cut into bite-sized chunks
$^1/_2$ to 1 tablespoon sugar
1 teaspoon salt
$^1/_2$ cup (125 ml) water

1 Heat the oil in a large stockpot over medium–low heat. Add the pumpkin and cook, stirring occasionally, until all the pumpkin is coated with oil and begins to soften.
2 Add the sugar, salt and water and cover the pot. Reduce the heat to low and cook for about 20 minutes, or until tender, stirring occasionally to prevent sticking. Remove from the heat and serve hot or at room temperature.

Serves 4
Preparation time: 10 mins
Cooking time: 30 mins

Okra with Tangy Ginger Dressing

10 oz (300 g) okra,
  washed
Fresh basil or Chinese
  celery leaves

Tangy Ginger Dressing
4 cloves garlic, minced
1 teaspoon grated ginger
$^1/_2$ teaspoon salt
1 teaspoon sugar
$1^1/_2$ teaspoons black
  Chinese vinegar
1 teaspoon soy sauce
1 tablespoon sesame oil

1 Bring a large pot of water to a rolling boil, then add
the okra. Return to a boil, cover, and reduce the heat
to low. Cook for 3 to 4 minutes, until the okra turns a
shiny dark green. Remove from the heat and drain
well in a colander.

2 To make the Tangy Ginger Dressing, place all the
ingredients, except the sesame oil, in a small bowl.
Slowly dribble in the sesame oil while beating
continuously with a whisk or a fork until the Tangy
Ginger Dressing is well blended.

3 Arrange the cooked okra on a serving platter, then
pour the Dressing evenly over them, add the garnish
if using, and serve.

Serves 4
Preparation time: **10 mins**
Cooking time: **15 mins**

Green Beans with Coconut

12 oz (350 g) green
beans, cut into pieces
(about 2¹/₃ cups)
1 cup (250 ml) water
2 tablespoons oil
1 teaspoon mustard seeds
1 onion, thinly sliced
2 green finger-length
chilies, deseeded and
thinly sliced
¹/₂ teaspoon asafoetida
powder (optional)
¹/₂ teaspoon salt
1 teaspoon sugar
1 cup (100 g) fresh
grated coconut
¹/₂ cup (70 g) roasted
ground peanuts

1 Bring the water to a boil in a pan. Add the beans and
return to a boil. Cook for 1 minute. Remove from the
heat, drain the beans, and rinse in cold water. Drain
and set aside in a mixing bowl.
2 Heat the oil in a separate pan. Add the mustard seeds
and fry until they pop. Add the onion and chilies and
stir-fry for 1 minute or until the onion softens.
4 Remove from the heat, add the asafoetida powder
and mix well. Combine with the beans, add all the
remaining ingredients and mix well. Serve with rice.

Serves 4
Preparation time: 20 mins
Cooking time: 10 mins

Squash with Tangy Sesame Dressing

2 lbs (900 g) summer
squash, zucchini or
pumpkin, peeled,
deseeded and cut into
chunks
2 oz (60 g) dried bean
thread noodles, soaked
10 minutes, drained,
and cut into lengths
(see note)
1 bell pepper, deseeded
and thinly sliced
1 tablespoon sesame
seeds, dry roasted
Chili oil, to garnish
(optional)

Tangy Sesame Dressing
3 teaspoons soy sauce
2 teaspoon black
Chinese vinegar
$1/2$ teaspoon freshly-
ground black pepper
$1/2$ teaspoon salt
1 to $1^1/_2$ teaspoons
sugar
2 teaspoons sesame oil

1 Place a steamer rack in a saucepan. Arrange the
pumpkin chunks on a heatproof plate and set on the
rack. Cover the steamer tightly and steam the pumpkin
over medium heat for 25 minutes. Remove the pumpkin
from the steamer. When cool enough to handle, cut
the pumpkin into thin strips, set aside.

2 Stir together all the Tangy Sesame Dressing ingredients,
except the sesame oil. Using a whisk or fork, beat in
the sesame oil until well blended.

3 Place the pumpkin strips and thinly sliced bell
pepper in a large salad bowl. Stir the Tangy Sesame
Dressing again to blend, and pour it evenly over
the vegetables.

4 Transfer to a smaller serving dish, sprinkle with the
ground sesame seeds, and drizzle with chili oil, if using.

Bean thread noodles, also known as "cellophane" or
"glass" noodles, are thin, clear strands made from
mung bean starch and water. Soak in hot water for
15 minutes to soften. Available from Asian food stores.

Serves 4–6
Preparation time: 35 mins
Cooking time: 40 mins

Crunchy Vegetables with Sesame Dressing

10 oz (300 g) fresh lotus root, washed and peeled
1$\frac{1}{2}$ cups (150 g) green beans, tops and tails removed, halved
1 teaspoon salt
1 carrot, peeled and sliced
$\frac{1}{2}$ cup (80 g) fresh or frozen green peas
1 stalk celery, sliced

Sesame Dressing
3 tablespoons vegetarian mushroom oyster sauce (see note)
2 cloves garlic, minced
1 teaspoon sesame oil
2 teaspoons dark sesame paste or tahini
$\frac{1}{2}$ teaspoon salt

Serves 4
Preparation time: **30 mins**
Cooking time: **50 mins**

1 Place the lotus roots in a pot and add 8 cups (2 liters) water. Bring to a full boil, cover, reduce the heat to low, and cook for 40 minutes. Remove from the heat, drain the lotus roots, and reserve the stock. Rinse the lotus roots in cool water, drain, and set aside to cool. When cool enough to handle, slice the lotus roots into round slices about $\frac{1}{4}$ in (6 mm) thick.
2 Bring the lotus stock to a boil and blanch the beans until they turn dark and shiny, about 2 minutes. Remove from the heat, drain, and rinse the beans in cool water. Drain and set aside to cool. Discard the stock.
3 Bring a cup of water with the salt to a boil in a saucepan. Add the carrots and blanch for 3 minutes; remove, rinse and set aside. Add the peas and celery, and cook for 1 minute; remove, rinse, and set aside.
4 In a large bowl, combine the Sesame Dressing ingredients, stirring well. Add all the vegetables and toss together until well coated. Transfer to a smaller salad bowl or platter and serve.

Vegetarian mushroom oyster sauce is a soy-based sauce that is the vegetarian substitute for regular oyster sauce.

Winter Melon with Ginger

Winter melon has always been a favorite Chinese food, not only for its succulence and fresh flavor, but also for its cooling properties—which soothe the digestive system by counterbalancing the heating properties of meat, chili, garlic, and other ingredients. Winter melon quickly absorbs the taste of whatever seasonings are added to it, so keep the flavorings to a minimum.

3 tablespoons oil
2 in (5 cm) fresh ginger, grated
1 small winter melon (2 lbs/900 g), peeled, deseeded and sliced
1 teaspoon salt
1 tablespoon sugar
$^1/_2$ cup (125 ml) water

1 Heat the oil in a wok over high heat and stir-fry the ginger and winter melon. Continue stir-frying until all the winter melon is coated with oil and the surface begins to soften, 3 to 5 minutes.
2 Add the salt, sugar, and water. Cover the wok, reduce the heat to medium, and cook for about 15 minutes, or until thoroughly tender. Transfer to a serving plate.

Serves 4
Preparation time: **15 mins**
Cooking time: **20 mins**

Five Spice Tofu Party Platter

Three large strips dried *konbu*, soaked in water for 40 minutes, rinsed and drained (see note)

2 cakes pressed tofu (*tau kwa*), about 10 oz/300 g each

1 carrot, peeled and sliced

16 dried black Chinese mushrooms, soaked in warm water for 20 minutes, stems discarded and caps sliced

1 daikon radish, peeled and cubed

$1/4$ cup (5 g) wood ear fungus, rinsed, soaked and drained, stems removed

1 in ($2^1/2$ cm) fresh ginger, grated

1 red finger-length chili, halved lengthwise

1 medium head broccoli, cut into florets

$1/2$ head iceberg lettuce, separated into leaves

Stock

4 cups (1 liter) water

$1/2$ tablespoon five spice powder (see note)

1 teaspoon salt

2 teaspoons sugar

2 tablespoons rice wine

$1/3$ cup (85 ml) soy sauce

Dips

Hot mustard

Soy sauce

Toasted sesame seeds

Sweet Thai chili sauce

1 To prepare the *konbu*, roll up each piece of soaked *konbu* to form a roll, then pierce it with a toothpick to secure and set aside.

2 To prepare the Stock, bring the water to a boil in a large pot. Add all the seasonings and return to the boil.

3 Add the tofu and all the vegetables to the Stock, except the broccoli and lettuce leaves. When it returns to a boil, cover and reduce the heat to low, and cook for 20 to 30 minutes. Stir gently once or twice to prevent sticking. After 20 minutes, add the broccoli. If the stock begins to evaporate, add a little more water.

4 Meanwhile, line a serving dish with the lettuce leaves. When the vegetables are tender, drain in a colander, reserving the stock. Discard the ginger and chili.

6 When cool enough to handle, cut the tofu squares and mushrooms into bite-sized pieces; remove the toothpicks from the seaweed rolls and cut each roll into bite-sized slices. Arrange all the cut ingredients on the serving dish.

7 Warm the Stock in a small saucepan and drizzle 2 tablespoons of the Stock evenly onto the cut vegetables and serve.

8 Serve with the hot Chinese or English mustard, soy sauce, toasted sesame seeds or sweet Thai chili sauce.

Five Spice Powder is a highly aromatic blend of Sichuan pepper, cinnamon, clove, fennel and star anise, ground to a fine powder.

Konbu or dried kelp is a type of seaweed commonly used in Japanese cooking. It has a dark brown color, often with whitish patches of salt, and is sold in strips or small folded sheets. Look for konbu in the Japanese section of supermarkets.

Serves 4
Preparation time: **20 mins + 40 mins soaking time**
Cooking time: **1 hour 20 mins**

Corn Kernels with Peanuts and Thai Chili Paste

$^{1}/_{2}$ cup (50 g) freshly grated coconut

5 to 6 corn cobs, or two 13-oz (370-g) cans of corn kernels, drained

1 cup (250 ml) water

$^{1}/_{2}$ tablespoon Thai chili paste (*nam prik pao*)

2 tablespoons soy sauce

2 tablespoons freshly-squeezed lime juice

1 teaspoon sugar

$^{1}/_{4}$ cup (50 g) roasted peanuts, coarsely ground

$^{1}/_{4}$ cup (60 ml) coconut milk

2 sprigs coriander leaves (cilantro), coarsely chopped

1 Dry roast the grated coconut in a skillet over low heat, about 10 minutes, until golden brown.

2 Steam or boil the corn until tender, around 6 to 8 minutes. Set aside to cool. Once cool, cut the kernels from the cobs. If using canned corn, heat the corn kernels in the water over medium heat until hot, about 10 minutes. Drain and set aside.

3 In a large mixing bowl, combine all the ingredients and stir well. Serve on individual plates or arrange in a large serving bowl.

Thai chili paste (*nam prik pao*) is a rich chili paste made from chilies, shallots, garlic, sugar, dried shrimp, fish sauce and tamarind.

Serves 4 to 6
Preparation time: 10 mins   Cooking time: 20 mins

Lotus Root with Green Onion and Sesame Seeds

2 fresh lotus roots,
(about 8 oz/250 g
each), sliced into pieces
1 tablespoon oil
2 green onions (scallions),
thinly sliced
1 teaspoon salt
$^1/_2$ teaspoon sugar
(optional)
$^1/_2$ cup (125 ml) water
1 tablespoon toasted
sesame seeds

1 Wash the lotus roots well and slice them crosswise into round pieces about $^1/_4$ in ($^1/_2$ cm) thick.
2 Heat the oil in a wok over high heat and when hot, stir-fry the lotus, green onions, salt, and sugar for 2 to 3 minutes.
3 Pour in the water, cover, and reduce the heat to medium, cooking for 5 more minutes. Transfer to a serving dish and garnish with the toasted sesame seeds.

Serves 4
Preparation time: **20 mins**
Cooking time: **10 mins**

Garlic Ginger Eggplant Stir-fry

Chinese cooks usually prepare eggplant with strong seasonings, simmered in richly flavored sauces. This makes the dishes an excellent accompaniment for rice and congee. Leftovers keep well overnight in the refrigerator and may be reheated the next day for lunch.

4 Asian eggplants (about 1$^1/_2$ lbs/700 g)
3 tablespoons oil
6 cloves garlic, minced
6 slices fresh ginger, minced
3 green onions (scallions), finely chopped
1 tablespoon chili paste
4 tablespoons water

Sauce
2 tablespoons soy sauce
1 tablespoon rice wine
$^1/_2$ to 1 tablespoon sugar
1 teaspoon vinegar
$^1/_2$ teaspoon salt
1 teaspoon sesame oil

1 Halve the eggplants lengthwise, then cut each half into 2 in (5 cm) pieces.

2 Combine all the Sauce ingredients in a bowl and set aside.

3 Heat the oil in a wok over high heat and when hot, add the eggplants, garlic and ginger and stir-fry until the eggplants begin to soften, about 4 minutes.

4 Add the green onions and chili paste and cook for 2 minutes. Add the Sauce and stir to combine all the ingredients. Add the water and cover. Reduce the heat to low and cook for 5 to 6 minutes. Transfer to a serving dish.

Serves 4
Preparation time: **15 mins**
Cooking time: **35 mins**

Stir-fried Squash with Bean Curd Sauce

1 1/2 lbs (700 g) summer squash or winter melon
1 tablespoon oil
3 cloves garlic, minced
1 teaspoon minced fresh ginger
1 teaspoon cornstarch dissolved in 2 tablespoons water
1 green onion (scallion), cut into lengths, to garnish
1 red finger-length chili, deseeded and sliced, to garnish

Sauce
2 squares fermented beancurd (see note)
1/2 teaspoon salt
1 teaspoon sugar
1 teaspoon sesame oil
1/4 cup (60 ml) water

1 Peel the squash or winter melon, remove the seeds, and cut into large chunks lengthwise.
2 Combine all the Sauce ingredients, stirring to break up the beancurd, then set aside.
3 Heat the oil in a wok until smoking and stir-fry the garlic and ginger for 30 seconds.
4 Add the squash or winter melon, stir-fry 1 to 2 minutes, and stir in the Sauce. Cover, reduce the heat to low, and cook until soft, 4 to 5 minutes.
5 Add the cornstarch mixture to the squash, stir well, cover, and cook 1 more minute for the Sauce to thicken. Garnish with the green onions and chili.

Fermented beancurd is sold in bottles in most Asian markets. The beige-colored cubes are soft and creamy in texture, and taste like strong, salty cheese. Available plain or with sesame oil and chili—both types may be used for this recipe.

Serves 4
Preparation time: **10 mins**
Cooking time: **10 mins**

Stir-fried Vegetables with Chinese Mushrooms

6 dried black Chinese
mushrooms, soaked in
warm water for 20 min-
utes
3 cups (750 ml) water
1 head broccoli, cut into
florets
$1/2$ head cauliflower, cut
into florets
4 tablespoons oil
4 slices ginger, minced
1 clove garlic, minced
2 green onions (scal-
lions), cut into lengths
1 tablespoon rice wine
2 teaspoons soy sauce
1 teaspoon salt
1 teaspoon sugar
2 teaspoons sesame oil

1 Slice the soaked mushroom caps into thin strips
and discard the stems, reserving the soaking water.
2 Place the water in a covered pot and bring to a boil.
Add the broccoli and cauliflower florets and let the
water return to a full boil. Blanch the vegetables for
1 minute, then drain in a colander.
3 Heat the oil in a wok until smoking, and add the
ginger, garlic, green onions and mushrooms. Stir for
1 minute. Add the wine and soy sauce, and stir-fry
for 2 minutes.
4 Stir in the vegetables, and season with the salt, sugar,
sesame oil, and 2 tablespoons of the mushroom soaking water. Cook for 2 more minutes and serve.

Serves 4
Preparation time: 20 mins + 20 mins soaking time
Cooking time: 15 mins

Carrot, Daikon and Mushrooms with Black Bean Paste

This tasty blend of vegetables, seasoned with fermented bean sauce, provides a wide range of nutrients and medicinal elements, and also provides a very attractive combination of colors and textures. If you prefer, you may use any variety of fresh mushroom in place of the dried black Chinese mushrooms. And if you like a hotter flavor, you may include a teaspoon of your favorite chili paste in the sauce mix. The dish goes well with rice, and may be used as a stuffing for various crêpes and pancakes, nori seaweed wraps, or fresh lettuce leaves.

$1/3$ cup (85 ml) oil
1 carrot, shredded
1 daikon radish, peeled and cut into matchsticks
5 dried black Chinese mushrooms, soaked in warm water for 20 minutes, stems discarded and caps sliced
1 leek, green top discarded, white bottom part sliced into quarters lengthwise, and cut into lengths
$1^1/_2$ tablespoons black bean paste (see note)
1 tablespoon rice wine
1 teaspoon sugar
$2/_3$ cup (60 g) fresh *enokitaki* or shiitake mushrooms, tough ends removed
2 tablespoons sesame oil
Fresh coriander leaves (cilantro), chopped

1 Heat the oil in a wok over high heat until smoking, and stir-fry the carrot, daikon, mushrooms and leek for 1 minute.

2 Season the vegetables with the bean sauce, wine, and sugar. Reduce the heat to medium–high, and cook for 4 to 5 minutes.

3 Add the mushrooms, stir-fry 1 to 2 minutes more, and stir in the sesame oil. Remove from the heat, garnish with the chopped coriander leaves, and serve.

Black bean paste is made from fermented soybeans, and is an important seasoning in Asian dishes. It has a strong, salty flavor and is available from Asian food stores.

Serves 4
Preparation time: 20 mins + 30 mins soaking time
Cooking time: 10 mins

Homestyle Chinese Scrambled Eggs

6 large eggs
1 teaspoon salt
1 teaspoon freshly-ground
  black pepper
1 teaspoon sugar
  (optional)
1 teaspoon soy sauce
1 onion, sliced into rings
3 tablespoons oil
3 tomatoes, cut into
  wedges

1 In a large bowl, beat the eggs well, then add the salt, pepper, sugar, soy sauce and onion. Continue beating until well blended.
2 Heat the oil in a wok over medium heat and when hot, add the beaten eggs. Scramble the egg mixture quickly with a spatula for 1 to 2 minutes, then add the tomatoes and continue to stir-fry until the eggs are uniformly cooked and dry. Transfer to a serving dish.

Serves 4
Preparation time: **5 mins**
Cooking time: **5 mins**

Eggs with Sweet Sambal Chili Sauce

8 to 10 dried chilies
4 red finger-length chilies, deseeded
6 shallots, peeled
4 tablespoons oil
2 teaspoons lime or lemon juice
1 to 1$\frac{1}{2}$ teaspoons sugar
1 teaspoon salt
4 hard-boiled eggs, shelled

Serves 4
Preparation time: **15 mins**
Cooking time: **20 mins**

1 Cut the dried chilies into short lengths and soak them in warm water to soften, about 10 to 15 minutes. Then deseed and drain.
2 Grind the dried and fresh chilies and shallots in a mortar or blender, adding a little oil if necessary to keep the blades turning.
3 Heat the oil in a wok over low heat and stir-fry the ground ingredients until the oil separates from the mixture, about 5 minutes. Add the lime or lemon juice, salt and sugar, and mix well.
4 Halve the eggs lengthwise and place on a serving dish. Spoon the cooked chili paste over the eggs and serve.

Some cooks deep-fry the shelled whole eggs before adding the chili paste as this gives them a crisp coating.

Sweet and Sour Pineapple Curry

2 tablespoons oil
5 shallots, sliced
2 cloves garlic, minced
1 stick cinnamon
4 cloves
1 star anise pod (see note)
3 cardamom pods, slit and bruised
1 fresh pineapple (about 2 lbs/1 kg), peeled and cut in bite-sized chunks
$^2/_3$ cup (80 g) finely chopped palm sugar or dark brown sugar
2 red finger-length chilies
1 cup (250 ml) thin coconut milk
1 teaspoon salt
2 green finger-length chilies, sliced length-wise

Spice Paste
1 tablespoon coriander seeds
$^1/_2$ teaspoon cumin seeds
$^1/_2$ teaspoon fennel seeds
5 shallots, peeled
2 cloves garlic, peeled
1 red finger-length chili
$^1/_2$ in (1 cm) turmeric root, peeled and sliced, or $^1/_2$ teaspoon ground turmeric
$^1/_2$ teaspoon salt

1 Prepare the Spice Paste by dry-frying the coriander seeds, cumin, and fennel in a skillet over low heat until fragrant, about 3 minutes. Transfer to a blender or spice grinder and grind to a fine powder. Add the shallots, garlic, chilies, turmeric and salt to the spice grinder or blender and grind to form a smooth paste. Add a little oil, if needed, to keep the mixture turning. Set aside.

2 Heat the oil in a saucepan, add the shallots and garlic, and stir-fry over medium heat until golden brown, 1 to 2 minutes. Add the Spice Paste, cinnamon, cloves, star anise, and cardamom. Stir-fry until fragrant, 3 to 4 minutes. Add the pineapple, sugar and red chilies, and cook over low to medium heat for 5 minutes, stirring frequently.

4 Add the thin coconut milk, bring to a boil. Reduce the heat to low and simmer, uncovered, for 5 minutes. Add the green chilies and cook until the pineapple is soft, 2 to 3 minutes. Transfer to a serving dish.

Star anise is a dark brown, strongly-flavored spice that resembles an eight-pointed star. Its aroma is similar to anise or cinnamon. Store in a tightly-sealed jar in a cool, dry place.

Adjust the amount of sugar used according to the sourness of the pineapple used.

Serves 4 to 6
Preparation time: 20–25 mins
Cooking time: 20 mins

Eggplant Curry

1/2 cup (100 g) mung dal, washed and drained
1/2 teaspoon ground turmeric
1 teaspoon ghee or oil
2 cups (500 ml) water
2 Asian eggplants or 1 large globe eggplant (about 10 oz/300 g), cubed
1 teaspoon ground cumin
2 teaspoons ground red pepper
1/4 cup (75 g) tamarind pulp mixed with 1 cup (250 ml) water, mashed and strained for juice
1 1/4 teaspoons salt
2 tablespoons oil
1 teaspoon urad dal
1/2 teaspoon mustard seeds
1 teaspoon cumin seeds
1/2 teaspoon fennel seeds, coarsely ground
1 onion, finely sliced
2 sprigs curry leaves
2 tablespoons coriander leaves (cilantro), finely chopped

1 Place the mung dal, turmeric, ghee or oil and water in a pan, bring to a boil, and simmer over medium heat, until the dal is cooked, about 10 minutes.

2 Add the eggplant, cumin and ground red pepper, tamarind juice and salt. Cook until the eggplant is tender, about 8 minutes.

3 In a separate pan, heat the oil and stir-fry the urad dal until golden brown about 4 minutes. Add the mustard, cumin and fennel. Fry until aromatic, about 2 minutes.

4 Add the onion and curry leaves and stir-fry until the onion becomes golden brown.

5 Transfer the spice-onion mixture to the eggplant curry. Add the chopped coriander leaves and cook for 2 minutes more. Remove from the heat and serve.

Serves 4–6
Preparation time: 15 mins
Cooking time: 25 mins

Curried Bell Peppers

2 large or 3 medium bell peppers
2 tablespoons oil
1 teaspoon fennel seeds
1/2 teaspoon cumin seeds
4 cardamom pods
1 onion, thinly sliced
1 can (14 oz/400 g) whole tomatoes
2 tablespoons ginger, paste (see note)
1 tablespoon garlic paste (see note)
1 tablespoon sesame seeds, dry-roasted
2 teaspoons ground red pepper
2 teaspoons ground coriander
1/2 teaspoon ground turmeric
1 teaspoon *garam masala*
1 1/4 teaspoons salt
1 teaspoon sugar
1 teaspoon lime juice or vinegar
1/4 cup (60 ml) water

1 Deseed the bell peppers and slice thinly lengthwise.
2 Heat the oil in a wok or large skillet over medium heat and stir-fry the fennel, cumin seeds, and cardamoms until fragrant. Add the onion slices and stir-fry until golden brown.
3 Add the tomatoes, ginger and garlic pastes, sesame seeds, chili, ground coriander and turmeric, and *garam masala*. Reduce the heat to low and cook for 10 minutes or until the oil separates.
4 Add the bell peppers and the remaining ingredients. Mix well, cover and cook until the bell peppers are soft, about 5 minutes. Serve hot.

Garlic or ginger paste can be prepared by blending or pounding the required amount of garlic or ginger needed with some water. A garlic press may also be used. Since these pastes are used in many of the recipes in this book, you may prefer to make a large batch in advance it in the refrigerator.

Serves 4–6
Preparation time: 25 mins
Cooking time: 20 mins

Curried Pumpkin

2 tablespoons oil
$1/2$ teaspoon mustard seeds
1 teaspoon fennel seeds
$1/4$ teaspoon fenugreek (see note)
$1/2$ teaspoon dried chili flakes
1 onion, sliced
1 green finger-length chili, deseeded and cubed
$1/2$ pumpkin or 1 butternut squash (about $1 1/2$ lbs/700 g), deseeded, peeled and cubed
1 cup (250 ml) water
1 teaspoon ground turmeric
1 teaspoon ground red pepper
1 teaspoon ground cumin
$1 1/2$ teaspoons salt
$1/4$ cup (75 g) tamarind pulp mixed with $1/2$ cup (125 ml) water, mashed and strained for juice
$1/2$ cup (60 g) caster sugar

1 Heat the oil in a large skillet and stir-fry the mustard and fennel seeds, fenugreek and dried chilies until the chilies turn brown. Add the onion and green chilies and stir-fry for 2 minutes or until the onion turns golden brown.

2 Add the pumpkin, water, ground red pepper, ground cumin and turmeric, and salt. Cover and cook over medium heat until the pumpkin pieces are almost tender, about 15 minutes.

3 Add the tamarind juice and sugar and cook until the liquid is absorbed and the pumpkin is soft.

Fenugreek is a small almost square, hard, yellowish-brown seed. The seeds are strongly flavored and are easily available from Asian foodstores and supermarkets. The taste of the spice is somewhat like burnt maple, sweet yet bitter with a hint of celery. In addition to curries, fenugreek will enhance meats, poultry and vegetables. Too much of it will cause foods to become bitter, however, so use with caution until you become familiar with it.

Serves 4–6
Preparation time: **15 mins**
Cooking time: **25 mins**

Curried Potatoes with Stuffing

4 large potatoes, peeled
2 tablespoons oil
2 onions, diced
1 in (2$^1/_2$ cm) ginger
2 cloves garlic
3 tomatoes, sliced
1 onion, finely sliced
$^1/_2$ teaspoon ground
  cumin
1 teaspoon ground
  turmeric
1 teaspoon *garam masala*
$^1/_2$ teaspoon ground red
  pepper
3 tablespoons yogurt
3 tablespoons coconut
  milk or milk
1 cup (250 ml) water
1$^1/_4$ teaspoons salt
Fresh coriander leaves
  (cilantro), chopped

Stuffing
$^1/_3$ cup (30 g) raw
  almonds, blanched and
  chopped
$^1/_3$ cup (30 g) raw
  cashew nuts, chopped
$^1/_3$ cup (30 g) raw pista-
  chio nuts, chopped
$^1/_2$ cup (80 g) raisins,
  chopped
3 tablespoons sour cream
  or yogurt
1 teaspoon ground red
  pepper
Pinch of salt

1 Boil the potatoes until partially cooked, about 10 minutes, then halve them. Scoop out some of the insides with a spoon, leaving about a $^1/_4$-in ($^1/_2$-cm) thick shell of potato.

2 Mix the scooped potato flesh with all the Stuffing ingredients. Place 1 tablespoon of the Stuffing back into each potato half. Tie the two halves of the stuffed potatoes with a kitchen string and set aside.

3 Heat the oil and stir-fry the diced onion until golden brown. Combine the fried onion with the ginger, garlic and tomatoes and grind in a blender to form a paste.

4 Heat the oil and stir-fry the sliced onion until golden brown. Add the blended ingredients and the spices—cumin, turmeric, masala, and ground red pepper. Stir-fry over low heat until the oil separates.

5 Add the yogurt, milk, water, and salt. Bring to a boil and cook for 3 minutes. Add the potatoes and continue to cook for another 5 minutes.

6 Cover and cook until the gravy becomes thick and coats the stuffed potatoes. Garnish with the coriander leaves and serve.

Serves 4
Preparation time: 15 mins
Cooking time: 45 mins

Curried Peas and Mushrooms with Cashews

2 tablespoons ghee or oil
1 cinnamon stick, broken in two
5 whole cloves
5 cardamom pods
1 onion, thinly sliced
1 1/2 tablespoons ginger paste (see note)
1 1/2 tablespoons garlic paste (see note)
1 can (14 oz/400 g) whole tomatoes
2 tablespoons ground coriander
1 tablespoon ground red pepper
1 teaspoon ground turmeric
2 teaspoons *garam masala*
1 1/2 teaspoons salt
1 1/2 cups (375 ml) water
2 cups (200 g) button mushrooms, sliced
1 1/2 cups (225 g) fresh or frozen green peas
2/3 cup (80 g) raw cashew nuts blended with 1/2 cup (125 ml) water until smooth
1 1/2 tablespoons tomato purée
2 tablespoons chopped coriander leaves (cilantro)

1 Heat the ghee or oil in a skillet and stir-fry the cinnamon sticks, cloves and cardamom until aromatic. Add the sliced onion and stir-fry until golden brown.
2 Add the ginger and garlic pastes and stir-fry for 1 minute. Add the tomatoes, and coriander, chili, ground turmeric and *garam masala*. Cook over low heat until the oil separates, about 5 minutes .
3 Add the salt and water and bring to a boil. Add the mushrooms, green peas, blended cashew nuts and tomato purée.
4 Cover and cook for 5 minutes, stirring occasionally. Remove from the heat and sprinkle with the chopped coriander leaves before serving.

Garlic or ginger paste can be prepared by blending or pounding the required amount of garlic or ginger needed with some water. A garlic press may also be used. Since these pastes are used in many of the recipes in this book, you may prefer to make a large batch in advance it in the refrigerator.

Serves 4–6
Preparation time: 25 mins
Cooking time: 15 mins

Curried Potatoes in Coconut Milk

2/3 cup (80 g) raw
cashew nuts
3/4 cup (180 ml) milk or
coconut milk
2 tablespoons ghee or oil
1 cinnamon stick, broken
in two
6 cardamom pods
6 whole cloves
1 teaspoon fennel seeds,
coarsely pounded
2 onions, finely chopped
2 sprigs curry leaves
4 tablespoons curry
powder
2 tablespoons ginger
paste (see note)
2 tablespoons garlic paste
(see note)
5 cups (1 1/4 liters) water
1 cup (100 g) sliced fresh
button mushrooms
2 potatoes, peeled and
diced
1 carrot, diced
2 tomatoes, diced
1 cup (50 g) fresh or
frozen peas
1 1/2 teaspoons salt
2 tablespoons chopped
coriander leaves
(cilantro)
1 tablespoon freshly-
squeezed lime juice

1 In a blender, blend the cashew nuts and milk until very smooth. Set aside.

2 Heat the ghee or oil in a wok over medium heat and stir-fry the cinnamon, cardamoms, cloves and fennel seeds until aromatic. Add the onion and curry leaves and stir-fry for 2 minutes until golden brown.

3 Mix the curry powder with the ginger and garlic pastes, add to the pan, reduce the heat to low, and cook until the oil separates, about 2 minutes.

4 Add the water, mushrooms, diced vegetables, peas and salt. Cover and cook over medium heat until the vegetables are cooked, about 15 minutes. Two minutes before the end of cooking add the cashew nut mixture.

5 Remove from the heat and stir in the coriander leaves and lime juice.

Garlic or ginger paste can be prepared by blending or pounding the required amount of garlic or ginger needed with some water. A garlic press may also be used. Since these pastes are used in many of the recipes in this book, you may prefer to make a large batch in advance it in the refrigerator.

Serves 4–6
Preparation time: 25 mins
Cooking time: 25 mins

Potato and Chickpea Curry

1 can cooked chickpeas (also known as garbanzo beans), drained and rinsed
1 to 2 tablespoons oil
2 potatoes, peeled and diced
2 tablespoons ghee or oil plus extra oil for frying
1 teaspoon cumin seeds
2 bay leaves
1 onion, thinly sliced
2 tomatoes, thinly sliced
2 tablespoons ground coriander
1 tablespoon ground cumin
2 tablespoons ground red pepper
1 teaspoon ground turmeric
2 teaspoons *garam masala*
1 1/2 teaspoons salt
1 1/2 cups (375 ml) water
1 1/2 tablespoons lime or lemon juice
1 tablespoon finely sliced ginger strips
2 tablespoons chopped coriander leaves (cilantro)

1 Place the soaked chickpeas in a pan and add sufficient water to cover. Bring to a boil, and cook until the chickpeas are tender, about 30 minutes. Drain and set aside. (If using canned chickpeas, use straight from the can after rinsing.)

2 Heat the oil in a skillet. Fry the diced potatoes until golden brown. Remove and drain on paper towels.

3 Heat the ghee or oil in a wok over medium heat. Add the cumin seeds and bay leaves and stir-fry until aromatic. Add the onion slices and stir-fry over low heat until the onion turns golden brown, about 5 minutes.

4 Add the tomatoes, ground coriander, cumin, chili and turmeric, *garam masala* and salt, and stir-fry over very low heat until the oil separates.

5 Add the chickpeas, fried potatoes and the water. Bring to a boil and cook for 5 minutes. Remove from the heat.

6 Stir in the lime juice, strips of ginger and coriander leaves before serving.

To avoid frying, add the cubed potatoes to the pan of boiling chickpeas after 15 minutes (Step 1).

Serves 4–6
Preparation time: **20 mins + 5 hours soaking time**
Cooking time: **40 mins**

Yellow Lentil 'Meatball' Curry

1½ cups (300 g) tur dal, soaked for 3 hours
3 tablespoons channa dal, soaked for 3 hours
2 green finger-length chilies, cut into lengths
½ teaspoon ground turmeric
½ teaspoon asafoetida powder (optional)
½ teaspoon salt
1 cup (100 g) finely grated carrot
4–6 dried red chilies, soaked
¾ teaspoon fenugreek
¼ cup (75 g) tamarind pulp mixed with 4 cups (1 liter) water, mashed and strained to obtain juice
2 tablespoons oil
1 teaspoon cumin seeds
½ teaspoon mustard seeds
2 sprigs curry leaves

1 Drain both the tur and channa dals and grind them to a paste in a blender or food processor with the green chilies, ground turmeric, asafoetida and salt (it may be easier to do this in several batches). Stir in the grated carrot and mix well.

2 Shape the ground mixture into small balls and place on a lightly oiled tray. Steam for 10 minutes. Remove from the steamer and set aside.

3 Grind the dried chilies and fenugreek with the tamarind juice in a blender and set aside.

4 In a saucepan, heat the oil and stir-fry the cumin, mustard and the curry leaves until aromatic.

5 Add in the tamarind juice mixture, bring to a boil, then reduce the heat and simmer for about 10 minutes.

6 Add the steamed dal balls. Return to the boil and simmer for a further 5 minutes.

Fenugreek is a small almost square, hard, yellowish-brown seed. The seeds are strongly flavored and are easily available from Asian foodstores and supermarkets. The taste of the spice is somewhat like burnt maple, sweet yet bitter with a hint of celery. In addition to curries, fenugreek will enhance meats, poultry and vegetables. Too much of it will cause foods to become bitter, however, so use with caution until you become familiar with it.

Serves 4
Preparation time: 30 mins + 3 hours soaking time
Cooking time: 25 mins

Chickpea Curry with Crisp Indian Pancakes

This delicious chickpea curry is just one of the many vegetable or meat curries that make an excellent accompaniment to Roti Canai (see following page).

$^1/_2$ cup (100 g) channa dal (split chickpeas), washed
$3^1/_2$ cups (875 ml) water
$^1/_4$ teaspoon ground turmeric
1 onion, diced
1 carrot, peeled and sliced
1 Asian eggplant, cubed
1 tomato, cut into wedges
2 green finger-length chilies, cut into lengths
1 tablespoon tamarind pulp soaked in $^1/_2$ cup (125 ml) warm water, and strained to obtain juice
Scant $^1/_2$ cup (100 ml) coconut milk or milk
Salt, to taste
3 tablespoons oil
$^1/_2$ teaspoon black mustard seeds (see note)
$^1/_2$ teaspoon cumin seeds
1 sprig curry leaves
1 dried red chili, cut into short lengths
3 shallots, thinly sliced
3 cloves garlic, thinly sliced

1 Rinse and discard any grit from the dal. Place them in a pan with the water and turmeric, and bring to a boil over high heat. Reduce the heat to low and simmer for 20 minutes.

2 Add the onion, carrot, eggplant and tomato, and cook for 15 minutes until the vegetables are almost tender. Add the green chilies and cook for 5 minutes.

3 Add the tamarind juice, coconut milk and salt, and cook for 5 minutes.

4 Meanwhile, heat the oil in a skillet over medium heat, and stir-fry the mustard and cumin seeds for 30 seconds until the mustard seeds pop. Add the curry leaves, dried chilies, shallots and garlic, and stir-fry until the shallots and garlic turn golden brown, about 2 to 3 minutes. Pour this mixture into the pan with the dal and stir to mix well. Cover, and remove from the heat. Serve hot with Roti Canai (page 104).

Black mustard seeds are small, round seeds that impart an almost nutty flavor to dishes. Do not substitute yellow mustard seeds as the flavor is different.

Serves 4
Preparation time: 30 mins
Cooking time: 50 mins

Crisp Indian Pancakes (Roti Canai)

Roti Canai, a Malaysian favorite, is a delicious crispy pancake that is enjoyed throughout the day. This is an unconventional way to make Roti Canai but it is easier than attempting to duplicate the skilful manoeuvres of a Roti Canai chef. Serve with Chickpea Curry (page 96) or a curry of your choice.

$^1/_2$ tablespoon oil, for frying

Dough 1
2 cups (300 g) plain flour
1 teaspoons salt
$^1/_2$ tablespoon sugar
3 tablespoons (20 g) softened butter or oil
1 egg, beaten
$^1/_4$ cup (60 ml) milk
3 tablespoons water

Dough 2
1 cup (150 g) plain flour
$^1/_4$ cup (65 g) softened butter or oil

Makes 10 *roti*
Preparation time: **30 mins**
Standing time: **1–2 hours**
Cooking time: **20 mins**

1 To make Dough 1, combine the flour, salt and sugar in a mixing bowl. Add the softened butter or oil and mix with your fingertips. Beat the egg and milk together in a measuring cup, then add enough water to make 1 cup (250 ml) of liquid.

2 Slowly add $^3/_4$ cup (180 ml) of the egg-milk mixture to the bowl. Mix to make a fairly soft, pliable dough. If the dough seems dry, add the remaining liquid a little at a time. Stop adding the liquid once the dough starts to bind.

3 Knead the dough well on a lightly-floured surface for 10 to 15 minutes until the dough is smooth and elastic. Shape into a thick roll and divide into 8 equal pieces.

4 Roll each piece of dough into a smooth ball. Coat generously with more softened butter or oil and set aside for 1 to 2 hours. To make Dough 2, combine the flour and butter or oil in a bowl and mix until the mixture forms a soft, smooth dough. Divide into 8 pieces and roll each piece into a ball. Cover with a clean cloth and set aside.

5 To make a *roti*, flatten one Dough 1 ball into a disc about 3 in $(7^1/_2$ cm) in diameter. Place one Dough 2 ball in the center of a disc and wrap it around the dough ball.

6 On a lightly-floured surface, use a rolling pin to roll the ball into a rectangle about 5 x $6^1/_4$ in (13 x 16 cm). Roll the dough up lengthwise.

7 Flatten the roll into a thin sheet again. Now roll it up from the short end to make a short, fat roll. Cut the roll into 2 equal halves.

8 Sit the dough on its side, then roll each piece out thinly with a rolling pin to get a thin disc (5 in/13 cm diameter) lightly marked with concentric circles.

9 Heat $^1/_2$ tablespoon of the oil on a griddle and cook the *roti* over medium heat for 2 to 3 minutes on each side until golden brown. Transfer to a flat surface and, using cupped hands, deftly press the *roti* from the outside towards the center a couple of times to fluff the layers. Serve hot with Split Chickpea Curry.

Green Beans and Sweet Potato Curry

10 oz (300 g) sweet pota-
toes, peeled and cubed
7 oz (200 g) green beans
cut into lengths
1 teaspoon ground
turmeric
1 teaspoon salt

3 cups (750 ml) water
1 cup (100 g) grated
fresh coconut
1 tablespoon ground cumin
2 green finger-length
chilies
4 sprigs curry leaves

$1/_2$ cup (125 ml) yogurt
2 tablespoons oil
1 teaspoon mustard seeds

Serves 4–6
Preparation time: 20 mins
Cooking time: 20 mins

1 Combine the plantain or sweet potato cubes, green beans, turmeric, salt and water
in a large saucepan and cook until the plantain or sweet potato is soft.
2 Meanwhile, grind the grated coconut, cumin, green chilies, two sprigs of the curry
leaves and yogurt together in a blender until smooth and set aside.
3 Heat the oil in a skillet. Fry the mustard seeds until they pop, then add the remaining
two sprigs of curry leaves. When aromatic, transfer to the boiling vegetables along
with the blended spices. Boil for 2 minutes, remove from the heat and serve.

Grated fresh coconut can be purchased from Asian markets or you can grate it yourself.
Purchase coconuts that are heavy and have a lot of juice in them. Crack IT open and drain
the juice. Break the shell into smaller pieces by turning over on a firm surface and knocking
with a mallet. Use a knife to release the meat from the shell. Remove the flesh from the
shell and peel the brown outer skin using a vegetable peeler. Grate the flesh in a blender
or food processor.

Spinach, Mushrooms and Tofu in Clear Broth

1 tablespoon oil
2 cloves garlic, minced
2 slices fresh ginger
2 cups (300 g) fresh spinach, washed and trimmed
3¹/₄ cups (800 ml) vegetable stock or water
1 cake soft tofu (about 10 oz/300 g), cubed
1 cup (100 g) fresh button or black Chinese mushrooms
2 teaspoons sesame oil
Salt and freshly-ground black pepper, to taste

1 Heat the oil in a wok until smoking, add the garlic and ginger, and stir-fry for 30 seconds. Add the spinach and stir-fry for about 2 minutes until wilted.
2 Add the vegetable stock, tofu and mushrooms, and cover the wok. Bring to a full boil, reduce the heat to low, and cook for 2 to 3 minutes.
3 Remove from the heat, stir in the sesame oil, salt and pepper to taste, and serve.

Serves 4
Preparation time: **10 mins**
Cooking time: **10 mins**

Green Pea and Tofu Soup

Black moss fungus or "angel hair" is known in China for its blood-building properties and as a tonic food that turns grey hair black again. Here, it's combined with soft tofu and green peas to make a tasty, nourishing soup.

4 cups (1 liter) vegetable stock or water
$1/2$ teaspoon salt
$1/4$ teaspoon freshly-ground black pepper
1 carrot, peeled and diced
1 cake soft tofu (about 10 oz/300 g), cubed
$1/2$ cup (50 g) fresh shiitake mushrooms, diced, or 5 dried black Chinese mushrooms, washed and soaked in warm water for 20 minutes, stems discarded and caps sliced
$1/2$ cup (80 g) fresh or frozen green peas
1 handful dried black moss fungus, washed and soaked 10 minutes in cool water (see note)
3 teaspoons cornstarch mixed with 3 tablespoons cool water
2 teaspoons sesame oil
1 cup (50 g) fresh mung bean sprouts, washed and trimmed
2 green onions (scallions), chopped, to garnish

1 Bring the stock or water and the salt and pepper to a full boil, and add the diced carrot and tofu cubes. Cover, reduce the heat to medium, and cook for 3 minutes.
2 Add the mushrooms, peas, and fungus to the soup, cover, and cook for another 2 minutes.
3 Stir the cornstarch mixture into the soup and it will thicken as it comes to a boil. Drizzle in the sesame oil, stir, and turn off the heat. Ladle into individual bowls, sprinkle the bean sprouts and green onions into each bowl and serve.

Black moss fungus, also known as "angel hair", is a fine, fiber-like fungus that is added to Chinese soups or used as a garnish in some Chinese dishes. It should be soaked in warm water until it becomes soft. If not available, use $1/2$ cup (60 g) dried bean thread noodles, soaked in hot water for 10 minutes to soften.

Serves 4
Preparation time: 5 mins + 10 mins soaking time
Cooking time: 20 mins

Thick Yogurt and Tomato Soup

$1/4$ cup (50 g) mung dal
5 cups ($1^1/4$ liters) water
2 ripe tomatoes, diced
1 teaspoon ground turmeric
1 teaspoon ground cumin
5 cloves garlic, finely minced
1 teaspoon peppercorns, coarsely pounded
2 tablespoons oil
$1/2$ teaspoon mustard seeds
2 dried red chilies, deseeded and sliced
1 teaspoon cumin seeds
$1/4$ teaspoon fenugreek (see note)
2 sprigs curry leaves
$1/2$ teaspoon asafoetida powder (optional)
$1^1/4$ teaspoons salt
1 cup (250 ml) plain yogurt mixed with $1/2$ cup (125 ml) water

Serves 4–6
Preparation time: 15 mins
Cooking time: 20 mins

1 Place the mung dal, water, tomatoes, ground turmeric and ground cumin in a pot, bring to a boil over medium heat and cook until the dal is very soft, about 15 minutes. Remove from the heat.

2 Using a sieve, strain the dal liquid into a bowl and set aside. Mash the dal thoroughly, then return to the soup liquid.

3 Add the garlic, cumin seeds and peppercorns. Return to a boil and simmer over medium heat for about 10 minutes.

4 Heat the oil in a separate pan and fry the mustard seeds, dried chilies, cumin seeds, fenugreek and the curry leaves until aromatic and the dried chilies turn brown. Add the asafoetida powder, then remove from the heat. Transfer to the simmering soup.

5 Add the salt, pour in the yogurt and mix well. Remove from the heat just as it begins to boil.

Fenugreek is a small almost square, hard, yellowish-brown seed. The seeds are strongly flavored and are easily available from Asian foodstores and supermarkets. The taste of the spice is somewhat like burnt maple, sweet yet bitter with a hint of celery. In addition to curries, fenugreek will enhance meats, poultry and vegetables. Too much of it will cause foods to become bitter, however, so use with caution until you become familiar with it.

Spicy Lentil Stew with Green Chilies

$^1/_2$ cup (100 g) tur dal, washed and drained
$^1/_4$ cup (50 g) mung dal, washed and drained
$^1/_4$ cup (50 g) masoor dal, washed and drained
4 teaspoons ghee or oil
5 cups (1$^1/_4$ liters) water
1 teaspoon ground turmeric
1$^1/_4$ teaspoons salt
1 teaspoon cumin seeds
1 onion, thinly sliced
2 green finger-length chilies, deseeded sliced
2 teaspoons ginger grated
2 tablespoons coriander leaves (cilantro), finely chopped
$^1/_4$ teaspoon asafoetida powder (optional)
$^1/_2$ teaspoon ground red pepper
1 tablespoon lemon juice

1 Place the tur, mung and masoor dal in a saucepan with 1 teaspoon ghee or oil, water, ground turmeric, and salt. Bring to a boil and cook for about 30 minutes.
2 Remove from the heat and, using the back of a spoon, mash the dal.
3 Heat 3 teaspoons ghee or oil in a separate pan. Add cumin seeds, cook them until they pop, and then add the onion, chilies, and ginger. Stir-fry until the onion is soft, then add the coriander leaves, asafoetida powder and ground red pepper. Stir to mix well and transfer to the mashed dal.
4 Return to the boil and cook for 3 minutes. Remove from the heat and stir in the lemon juice. Serve with rice.

Serves 4–6
Preparation time: 15 mins
Cooking time: 45 mins

Mixed Vegetable Stew with Curry Spices

2 tablespoons oil
2 tablespoons channa dal
2 tablespoons urad dal
2 green finger-length chilies, deseeded and chopped
10 cloves garlic, sliced
$1^1/_2$ tablespoons cumin seeds
$^1/_2$ cup (50 g) grated fresh coconut
1 teaspoon ground turmeric
1 cup (250 ml) water
1 cup (100 g) thinly sliced cabbage
1 carrot, peeled and cubed
1 cup (50 g) green beans, cut into pieces
8 oz (250 g) cauliflower, cut into small florets
1 cup (150 g) fresh or frozen green peas
$1^1/_4$ teaspoons salt
2 cups (500 ml) water
2 tablespoons ghee or oil
1 teaspoon cumin seeds
1 teaspoon mustard seeds
2 sprigs curry leaves

1 Heat the oil in a wok over medium heat and stir-fry the channa and urad dal until golden brown. Add the green chilies, garlic, cumin seeds, grated coconut and ground turmeric. Stir-fry until the coconut is a shade darker, about 5 minutes.
2 Cool the stir-fried ingredients and blend with 1 cup (250 ml) of water until smooth.
3 Put all the vegetables, salt and water into a pan along with the blended ingredients and cook over medium heat for about 15 minutes.
4 In a separate pan, heat the ghee or oil over medium heat, and stir-fry the cumin and mustard seeds, and the curry leaves until the mustard seeds pop.
5 Transfer the spices to the vegetable stew. Continue to simmer for about 5 minutes, then turn off the heat and serve.

Grated fresh coconut can be purchased from Asian markets or you can grate it yourself. Purchase coconuts that are heavy and have a lot of juice in them. Crack the coconut open and drain the juice. Break the shell into smaller pieces by turning over on a firm surface and knocking with a mallet. Use a knife to release the meat from the shell. Remove the flesh from the shell and peel the brown outer skin using a vegetable peeler. Grate the flesh in a blender or food processor, adding a bit of water to help the blades turn.

Serves 6
Preparation time: 25 mins
Cooking time: 30 mins

Curried Lentils with Spinach

1 cup (200 g) tur dal, washed and drained
5 cups (1 1/4 liters) water
1/2 teaspoon ground turmeric
2 green finger-length chilies, deseeded and slit lengthwise
4 cloves garlic
1 lb (500 g) spinach leaves, washed and chopped
1 teaspoon ground cumin
1/2 teaspoon ground red pepper
1 1/2 teaspoons salt
2 tablespoons ghee, or oil
1 teaspoon mustard seeds
1/2 teaspoon cumin seeds
1/2 teaspoon fennel seeds
2 dried chilies, cut into pieces
1 onion, thinly sliced
1/4 teaspoon asafoetida powder (optional)

1 Place the dal, water, ground turmeric, green chilies, and garlic cloves into a pan. Bring to a boil and cook over medium heat until the dal becomes soft, about 15 minutes.

2 Add the chopped spinach, cumin, ground red pepper and salt. Cover and cook until the spinach has wilted.

3 In a separate pan, heat the ghee or oil over medium heat and stir-fry the mustard, cumin and fennel seeds, and the dried chilies until the chilies turn light brown.

4 Add the onion and the asafoetida powder and stir-fry until the onion turns golden brown.

5 Transfer the fried spices and onion to the simmering dal. Cook for a further 2 minutes, then switch off the heat. Serve with rice or any kind of bread.

Serves 4–6
Preparation time: **15 mins**
Cooking time: **30 mins**

Tropical Mango Pudding

$^2/_3$ cup (150 ml) water
3 teaspoons gelatin
   powder (see note)
4 to 6 tablespoons
   superfine (caster) sugar
   (depending on the
   sweetness of the
   mangoes)
1 or 2 large ripe mangoes,
   about 14 oz (400 g)
$^2/_3$ cup (150 ml) milk
$^2/_3$ cup (150 ml)
   evaporated milk

Serves 6
Preparation time: 10 mins
Chilling time: 1 hour

1 Measure the water into a heatproof bowl and sprinkle the gelatin over the water. Set aside for 10 to 15 minutes until the gelatin absorbs the water and looks swollen and spongy. Melt the gelatin by setting the bowl in a larger bowl of hot water—stir until the gelatin is totally dissolved and there are no more lumps. Stir the sugar into the gelatin (if your mangoes are very sweet, you will need less sugar, if mangoes are a little sour, you need more).

2 Peel the mangoes and cut the mango flesh into small, neat dice to obtain 1 cup (5 oz/150 g) diced mango. Cut $1^1/_4$ cups (6 oz/180 g) of the remaining mango into rough cubes and purée in an electric blender or food processor with the fresh milk.

3 Combine the gelatin mixture, cream or evaporated milk, puréed mango and diced mango. Stir well and pour into small glass bowls. Chill well until set before serving.

Gelatin is an odorless, tasteless and colorless thickening agent that forms a jelly when dissolved in hot water and then cooled. Unlike agar-agar, it is made from boiled animal bones and tendons. Used in jellied desserts, salads and cold soups, gelatin is commonly sold in small packets of fine, white powder, although it is also sold in sheets or granules. Purchase unflavored gelatin for this recipe.

Sweet Corn Pudding

This corn pudding can be served turned out of its mold and surrounded by a spoonful of cream. Alternatively, you can also pour the hot pudding mixture into a glass dish or cake pan. After chilling, cut the pudding into squares and serve. Sliced pudding needs to be firmer to ensure easy cutting, so increase the quantity of mung bean flour from $1/2$ cup (60 g) to $2/3$ cup (80 g).

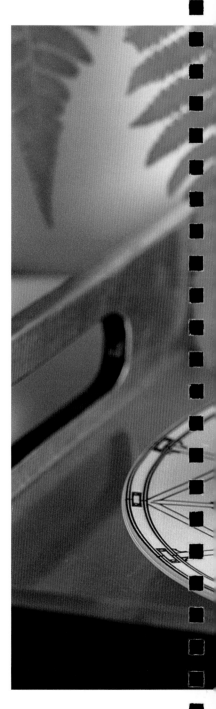

> $2^1/_2$ cups (600 ml) thin coconut milk
> $1/_2$ cup (60 g) mung bean flour
> $3/_4$ cup (180 g) sugar
> 1 teaspoon vanilla extract
> One 10-oz (300-g) can creamed corn

1 Combine the coconut milk, flour and sugar in a pan. Stir until well mixed. Add the vanilla extract and creamed corn.
2 Cook over low heat, stirring continuously with a wooden spoon, until the mixture boils and is thick and smooth. Allow the mixture to simmer for 3 to 4 minutes. Take the pan off the heat.
3 Spoon the mixture into 6 small jelly molds or bowls which have been rinsed with water. Leave the puddings to cool at room temperature before chilling in the refrigerator.
4 Sweetcorn pudding can be served turned out of its mold, surrounded by a spoonful of cream or evaporated milk.

Mung bean flour is made from ground roasted mung beans. Commonly mixed in with rice or wheat flour, it improves the texture of rice cakes and noodles. It can be purchased in small paper packets that come in various colors.

Serves 6 to 8
Preparation time: **10 mins**
Cooking time: **10 mins**

Yams and Bananas in Sweet Coconut Milk

2 sweet potatoes or yams, about 7 oz (200 g), peeled and cubed
A few drops vanilla extract
3 cups (750 ml) water
1 cup (250 ml) thick coconut milk
$1/2$ cup (100 g) sugar or chopped palm sugar
Pinch of salt
2 ripe bananas, peeled and cut diagonally

1 Place the sweet potato or yam in a medium saucepan with the vanilla extract and water and bring to a boil. Reduce the heat to medium and cook until the sweet potato is tender, 15 to 20 minutes.
2 Add the coconut milk, sugar, and salt and return to the boil. Add the sliced bananas and cook for a further 5 minutes. Serve warm or cold.

Sago Pearls may be added to give it an interesting texture. Rinse 1 tablespoon sago in a sieve and add at the end of step 2. Then cook the mixture for 5 minutes before adding the **coconut milk**.

Serves 5 to 8
Preparation time: 20 mins Cooking time: 30 mins

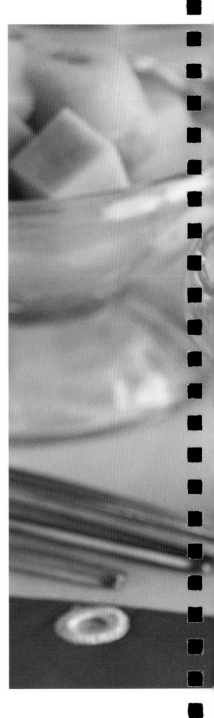

Shaved Ice with Palm Sugar Syrup

You need an ice-shaving machine to make this dessert properly. If you do not have one, replace with ice cubes ground in a blender, although this will make it more like a drink than the dessert that it is supposed to be. Cooked, sweetened azuki beans are sold in cans.

1 can (12 oz/350 g) cooked sweetened azuki beans
1 cup (200 g) seaweed jelly, diced (optional, see note)
One 10-oz (300-g) can of creamed corn
$^2/_3$ cup (150 ml) fruit-flavored or maple syrup
1 cup (250 ml) evaporated milk
Freshly shaved ice or crushed ice cubes

Palm Sugar Syrup
$^2/_3$ cup (150 ml) water
1 cup (200 g) shaved palm sugar or dark brown sugar

Serves 6
Preparation time: 10 mins
Assembling time: 10 mins

1 To make the Palm Sugar Syrup, place the water and palm sugar in a saucepan. Bring to a boil, then reduce the heat and simmer over medium heat until the sugar dissolves and the mixture becomes syrupy. Set aside to cool, then strain into a bowl.
2 To serve, place a generous spoonful of the azuki beans, seaweed jelly and corn in a deep serving bowl. Top with a mound of shaved ice and drizzle a spoonful each of the fruit and palm sugar syrups. Drizzle 1 to 2 tablespoons of the evaporated milk and serve immediately.

Azuki beans, or red kidney beans, are small dried beans often used in desserts. They are also cooked with sugar to make sweet red bean paste, which is sold in cans or jars. The dried beans and paste are sold in Asian markets.

Palm sugar (gula melaka) is made from the sap of the coconut or arenga palms. It is sold in rectangular or cylindrical blocks and ranges in color from gold to light brown with a strong caramel taste. Substitute brown sugar.

Seaweed jelly is considered to be very healthy. It is sold in cans in supermarkets.

Coconut Pumpkin Custard

1 small pumpkin (about 3 lbs/1 $^1/_2$ kgs), washed
4 eggs
1 $^1/_3$ cups (200 g) palm sugar, finely shaved with
  a knife
2 tablespoons sugar
Few drops vanilla essence
1 cup (250 ml) thick coconut milk
$^1/_2$ teaspoon ground cinnamon
$^1/_4$ teaspoon salt

1 Slice off the top of the pumpkin and reserve to use as a lid. Scoop out the seeds and fibers and discard. Wash, drain, and pat dry with paper towels. Replace the lid of the pumpkin and steam over boiling water for 15 minutes.
2 Place the eggs, palm sugar and sugar in a bowl and stir until the eggs are well mixed. Add the vanilla essence, coconut milk, cinnamon, and salt, and stir to mix thoroughly.
3 Pour the coconut milk mixture into the pumpkin, and cover with the lid. Place inside a steamer and steam over medium heat until the custard sets, 35 to 40 minutes. Remove the pumpkin and set aside to cool. Slice and serve at room temperature.

Serves 4 to 6
Preparation time: 20 mins
Cooking time: 1 hour

Sweet Red Date Soup with Lotus Seeds

This is both a popular Chinese dessert and a traditional herbal remedy for high blood pressure, arterioscelorsis, insomnia and immune defiency. All the ingredients are important items in the Chinese herbal pharmocopeia, and together they provide a potent tonic boost to the human energy system. According to Chinese lore, this soup should be served hot; eating it cold counteracts the medicinal benefits.

3 whole florets white (wood ear) fungus, soaked in cool water for 1 hour
30 dried white lotus seeds, soaked in cool water overnight (see note)
12 dried red dates or jujubes, washed and pits removed (see note)
6 cups (1^1/$_2$ liters) water
^{1}/$_2$ cup (75 g) rock crystal sugar

1 Drain the white fungus, trim, and discard the tough bases. Shred and set aside.

2 Drain the lotus seeds and place in a large pot with the red dates, white fungus and water.

3 Bring to a boil, and add the rock sugar. Cover, reduce the heat to low, and cook for 1 hour.

4 Adjust for sweetness, if necessary. Transfer the soup to a tureen or ladle into individual serving bowls. Serve hot.

Dried red dates, also known as Chinese jujubes, or *hong zao* in Mandarin, are the size of olives and although sour when raw, they are sweet when ripe and dried. Red dates are often eaten during Chinese New Year.

Lotus seeds can be seen at the tops of lotus pods as the pods ripen. They have a nutty flavor and are used in soups and stews. In some Asian countries, they are used to make desserts.

White fungus is also known as white wood ears, and has a crunchy texture and a slightly sweet flavor. It is sold dried and must be soaked in water before using.

Serves 4
Preparation time: overnight soaking
Cooking time: 1^1/$_2$ hours

Sweet Mung Bean Soup

If you prefer the soup chilled, let it cool after cooking, then put it in the refrigerator for a few hours prior to serving. Large quantities may be prepared in advance and kept for 4 to 5 days in the refrigerator. You may also flavor the soup by adding a cinnamon stick or some grated nutmeg to the water.

$1/_2$ cup (100 g) dried mung beans, picked clean and washed thoroughly (see note)
1 teaspoon vanilla extract
4 cups (1 liter) water
5 tablespoons sugar

1 Soak the mung beans overnight and drain. Place the beans and vanilla essence in a pan with 4 cups of water and bring to a boil. Reduce heat to medium–low and stir in the sugar. Cook until the beans are soft, about 45 minutes.
2 Adjust the sweetness, if necessary and serve in individual bowls.

Mung beans are small, green beans that reveal a yellow interior when the skins are removed (split). Mung beans are often used in desserts. They can be found in well-stocked supermarkets and health food stores.

Makes 4 small bowls
Preparation time: overnight soaking
Cooking time: 45 mins

Sweet Pumpkin and Lotus Seed Soup

For variation, you may add a cinnamon stick, split vanilla bean, or other aromatic spices to the soup while cooking. If you like the taste, try using $2/3$ cup (80 ml) of maple syrup for a sweetener in place of the rock sugar, or using $1/4$ cup (1 oz/37 g) rock sugar and $1/3$ cup (40 ml) maple syrup.

3 cups (345 g) diced pumpkin
8 cups (2 liters) water
1 floret white (wood ear) fungus, soaked in cool water for 1 hour
20 dried white lotus seeds, soaked overnight in cool water and drained (see note)
$1/2$ cup (75 g) rock crystal sugar
1 tablespoon cornstarch or water chestnut flour combined with 1 tablespoon water

1 Put the pumpkin cubes and water in a large pot, bring to a boil, then reduce the heat to medium.
2 Drain the white fungus and trim and discard the tough stems. Roughly shred and add the fungus, lotus seeds, and rock sugar to the pot. Cover and return to a boil, reduce the heat to low, and cook for 50 minutes.
3 Stir the cornstarch mixture, and add to the soup. Stir for 1 minute, cover, and cook for another 10 minutes. Remove from the heat and serve.

Lotus seeds can be seen at the tops of lotus pods as the pods ripen. They have a nutty flavor and are used in soups and stews. In some Asian countries, they are used to make desserts.

White fungus is also known as white wood ears, and has a crunchy texture and a slightly sweet flavor. It is sold dried and must be soaked in water before using.

Serves 4
Preparation time: **10 mins + overnight soaking**
Cooking time: **1$1/2$ hours**

Complete Recipe List